Transition to Success

by the same author

Supporting Young Transgender Men
A Guide for Professionals
ISBN 978 1 78592 294 7
eISBN 978 1 78450 601 8

of related interest

Transitions
Our Stories of Being Trans
Various Authors
Foreword by Sabah Choudrey, Juno Roche, and Meg-John Barker
ISBN 978 1 78775 851 3
eISBN 978 1 78775 852 0

Yes, You Are Trans Enough
My Transformation from Self-Loathing to Self-Love
Mia Violet
ISBN 978 1 78592 315 9
eISBN 978 1 78450 628 5

Trans Survival Workbook
Owl Fisher and Fox Fisher
ISBN 978 1 78775 629 8
eISBN 978 1 78775 630 4

The Trans Self-Care Workbook
A Coloring Book and Journal for Trans and Non-Binary People
Theo Lorenz
ISBN 978 1 78775 343 3
eISBN 978 1 78775 344 0

TRANSITION TO SUCCESS

A Self-Esteem and Confidence Workbook for Trans People

Matthew Waites

Jessica Kingsley Publishers
London and Philadelphia

First published in Great Britain in 2023 by Jessica Kingsley Publishers
An imprint of Hodder & Stoughton Ltd
An Hachette Company

1

Copyright © Matthew Waites 2023

All rights reserved. No part of this publication may be reproduced, stored in
a retrieval system, or transmitted, in any form or by any means without the
prior written permission of the publisher, nor be otherwise circulated in any
form of binding or cover other than that in which it is published and without
a similar condition being imposed on the subsequent purchaser.

Disclaimer: The information contained in this book is not intended to replace the
services of trained medical professionals or to be a substitute for medical advice.
You are advised to consult a doctor on any matters relating to your health, and in
particular on any matters that may require diagnosis or medical attention.

Content Warning: Discussion of weight loss.

The information in this book does not constitute financial advice, and neither the
publisher nor the author will be held responsible for any actions taken by readers pursuant
to the content in this book. For all financial matters that require decision making,
please consult with a trusted financial advisor or another professional on your own.

A CIP catalogue record for this title is available from the
British Library and the Library of Congress

ISBN 978 1 83997 051 1
eISBN 978 1 83997 052 8

Printed and bound in Great Britain by Bell and Bain Limited

Jessica Kingsley Publishers' policy is to use papers that are natural, renewable and recyclable
products and made from wood grown in sustainable forests. The logging and manufacturing
processes are expected to conform to the environmental regulations of the country of origin.

Jessica Kingsley Publishers
Carmelite House,
50 Victoria Embankment,
London, EC4Y 0DZ, UK

www.jkp.com

To Kathy,
Will you marry me?

Contents

Introduction

Identifying as transgender or gender diverse can be incredibly stressful and challenging; it can push you to experience a spectrum of emotions that many people don't. Challenges come from all areas of life – from work and education, society, media, family and friends – so it is clear to see why everyday life can be a struggle and reaching personal and life goals can seem out of reach. On my own journey of achievements, I've tried many different challenges and tools to push me towards my preferred future and have used the strategies within this book to do that. I've achieved things that I never thought would be possible, from publishing my first book (and now my second!), to having my dream job of working with LGBTQIA+ young people as well as owning my own business, scaling The Three Peaks and running half marathons, with much more in between! All of this was achieved using the strategies in this book and taking very small steps towards each of my goals. What I've learnt on my journey as a trans man has helped me to become who I am today. The many obstacles that being trans puts in front of us every day has taught me resilience first and foremost and to work through things one by one, moving a tiny step forward each day.

Navigating day-to-day life as a gender diverse person whilst simultaneously working on your personal development goals can be stressful and hard at times, but it is these challenging times that will teach you things about yourself that you didn't know existed. It will give you strength on your most challenging days, increase your resilience and improve relationships and your sense of self-worth. These are valuable attributes which will propel you into achieving things you've only dreamed of. It doesn't matter whether you're trying to make very small changes to your day-to-day life or if you've got dreams to run your own business and become self-employed; the strategies within this book are designed to support you no matter what your goals are.

Many people move through their lives maintaining their status quo, believing change is not possible and that aspirations cannot be achieved; but by incorporating the strategies outlined in this book, and committing to yourself and your goals, your preferred future can become your reality.

Use this book from a personal perspective, if you don't want to work on relationships, health or careers for example but would find self-esteem and confidence useful then you can concentrate on those sections. Your use of these strategies must be personalised for yourself to help you get to where you want to be.

We all have one thing in common: we are human beings. People who have achieved amazing things in their lives still share that with the rest of society. It is important to recognise that some people do have the upper hand within society from being born into rich families, being cisgender and white, for example, so the struggle for people from other backgrounds is significantly more challenging. Systemic barriers cause day-to-day issues for many people from different communities and this can have a detrimental affect on wellbeing.

Investing time and resources in yourself is one of the most powerful forms of self-care. Personal development isn't about being selfish or rising above others; it's about becoming a better version of yourself, enhancing your life for you and those around you. This is particularly important if you're trying to rid yourself of destructive habits that have a direct impact on others. This book is designed to support you to make changes on things that you can control as opposed to things that you cannot.

Whatever your goals are, this is the place to start. It won't be an easy journey, but the reward and satisfaction you'll get from committing to investing in yourself will support you to live the life you've always wanted. Success doesn't necessarily mean big house, fast cars and a lot of cash in the bank. Success is defined as being 'the accomplishment of an aim or purpose.' This means you've achieved success if you've accomplished what you set out to. You can't reach success if you're aiming for other people's success because you won't have accomplished what you set out to, you'll have accomplished what others have set out to. Trans joy is real and is achieved by focusing on self-care, grabbing opportunities that come your way and making the most of the time that you have.

Chapter 1

Understanding Yourself and Your Values

Understanding yourself and your identity is a soul-searching journey, and one that is incredibly personal. From identifying as transgender and understanding your intersecting identities, it is likely that a lot of that work has already been done and you now have a stronger sense of self because of it. This is something to be celebrated, it takes a lot of self-reflection, energy and time to truly understand yourself and this section is designed to support you to build on that and understand your values alongside your identity.

Our values are what define us as humans and are crucial to our identities. They are things that we feel are important to us and will also shape the decisions that we regularly make. Our values can change and develop over time as we start to learn more about the world around us and the impact that we have on those we love, as well as the impact on our lives, careers, health and wellbeing. If people aren't aware of their values, this can lead them to making daily choices for the benefit of others, for monetary reward, for a 'better future' that they might not even want or because it's the 'right' thing to do in relation to their current trajectory of life.

Understanding your core values and principles as a human has many benefits for your life. Knowing what is important to you will help inform the choices you make every day, and if you're making the choices that align with your values, you will feel a much stronger sense of fulfilment and happiness. Making choices daily based on anything other than your fundamental beliefs can lead you down a path you don't want to pursue, and you can end up chasing things that are not important to you. For example, this can happen a lot with high-powered, well-paid jobs. People work because the pay is good but hate their jobs. They continue like this for years so they can buy things that they don't care for or want, to impress people they don't like being around. They work in a job that they hate because they believe the monetary reward is worth the sacrifice of spending 80 hours a week deeply unhappy. They are likely very stressed as well as compromising their relationships with the people they love. It's important that you truly know what your values are and what you stand for to make choices that align with these and therefore lead to sustainable fulfilment – and not just chasing the cash. Money doesn't always make people happy.

For success to become a reality, you must first understand what success looks like for you, what it is that drives you every single day and what it is that motivates you to succeed both short term and long term. This comes first and foremost from understanding what your core principles are as a human. You need to know what your own set of values and standards are, because without them, how will you know you are moving in the right direction? It's crucial to understand your values and standards because if you are aiming for goals that are misaligned with these, or goals you think you should be working to because of societal expectations, for example, you're more likely to fail and ultimately not be happy. No one will have the motivation to achieve their longer-term goals if they are not what they genuinely want to achieve and they'll no doubt fail at the first hurdle.

Personal values

Personal values are the set of rules or principles by which we live: they help us identify what is important to us and inform every action, reaction and response to life. They help us interact with the world as well as governing and informing the decisions that we make daily.

If you are not living your life in line with your principles and beliefs, this can cause you to feel emotions such as shame, guilt and anxiety. If you are not feeling fulfilled by the current trajectory you are on, it might be because you are not living in accordance with your values. It is vital therefore that you understand what is important to you and that you start to bring this to the forefront of your decision making. Doing this will form the foundation for the change that you want to see in your life. Knowing and understanding your values will help you to make informed decisions. By making the right decision based on what's fundamentally important to you, you will be happier and more confident with the direction your life moves in.

Understanding your personal set of values and standards can be a daunting task, so it is important to approach this one step at a time. How do you eat an elephant? Piece by piece of course!

To identify what your values are start by thinking about three key questions which explore a time when you were happy, a time when you were proud of yourself and a time when you felt fulfilled.

Consider the following questions and write down your answers:

Describe a time in your life when you felt genuinely happy. Where were you?

Who was there? What were you doing? What was it that made you feel happiness in that moment?

....

....

....

....

....

Describe a time when you felt proud of what you were doing. Where were you? What had you achieved? Think about the defining points that made you feel pride. What did you accomplish? Was there anyone else with you? Was it something you had to work hard for?

....

....

....

....

....

Describe a time when you felt truly fulfilled. Consider when you felt truly whole and when you felt a sense of purpose in your life. What were you doing? Where were you? Where did you live? Who were you with? What were you working for or towards?

....

....

....

....

....

Considering these experiences, what other feelings do you associate with these reflections? How did you feel before, directly afterwards and a few days afterwards? Did this have a longer-term impact for you? Why did you pick these moments?

....

....

....

....

Now that you've considered what you were doing that made you feel happy, proud and fulfilled, were they all part of the same time in your life or were they different parts/different times/different scenarios? Were they linked in some way?

....

....

....

....

....

Considering these experiences, what values do you associate with these times in your life? To help you think about what these might be, here are some examples:

Authenticity	Compassion	Bravery	Challenge
Community	Creativity	Fairness	Education
Determination	Honesty	Generosity	Kindness
Leadership	Loyalty	Justice	Environmentalism
Respect	Self-respect	Status	Responsibility
Stability	Wisdom	Recognition	Growth
Fun	Citizenship	Passion	Efficiency
Dependability	Commitment	Positivity	Optimism
Fitness	Courage	Service to others	Genuine

Write down *all* the words that you feel reflect your own personal values here:

....

....

....

....

....

Are there any other values that you consider as being fundamental to you that you have not been able to identify above? Describe them here:

....

....

....

Now that you have identified the values that are important to you and those that appeared during experiences that were meaningful, it is important to understand what your core values are. Your core values will help carve out your path in life, determine the choices you make, and give you ownership and responsibility over them. They will also help you when you have a particularly challenging or difficult decision to make – they will help you do the right thing for you.

Narrow down your values as written above to your top ten:

1. ....

2. ....

3. ....

4. ....

5. ....

6. ....

7. ....

8. ....

9. ....

10. ....

To determine what your core values are, give them a score on a scale of 1 to 10, 1 being most important and 10 being least important. Place the score next to each of the values above.

Place your top-scoring value in the centre of the following diagram and your other four values in the spaces around it:

These are your core values: the values that are explicitly central to all that you do or want to do and will help to give you a sense of fulfilment on your path throughout life. If your behaviours or decisions aren't aligned with these values, that's when you feel the most conflict. Conflict within your life can contribute towards stress, anxiety, depression and a general feeling of not being complete. When your actions align with your values, you demonstrate to others that you have integrity, and this also supports you to improve and increase your levels of personal confidence.

You can complete this activity numerous times. Your core values might change over time, and if you are growing and learning, they should change over time. What is important to you at age 20 might not be as important when you are 40, for example.

> ### TOP TIP
> Review your values using the exercise above once every year. This will help you realign them if necessary, taking into account your learning along the way, and support you to achieve your next set of goals.

Personal values statement

To understand and embed your values and principles so that they are at the forefront of every decision you make, you can make a commitment to yourself by writing a personal values statement. Remember your values statement whenever you have a decision to make and ask yourself the fundamental question: does this decision align with my core values? This will inform all your decisions about every aspect of your life, from the small and everyday to the big, life-changing ones.

It is important to take time over writing this statement and take into consideration what you have learnt about yourself. This statement is a commitment to you and future you. When you use it, it should be watertight, because otherwise it will fail you when you are making choices and decisions that will affect which direction your life goes in next.

Your personal values statement will help give structure and guidance to your life on your journey to achieving your personal, professional and life goals. When writing it consider the following:

✦ Start with your values. Why are these important to you? What do you think these values bring to your life? How can your values influence others and create positive change?

✦ What are you committing to yourself? Who are you? Who do you want to be?

- How would your friends describe you now? How do your family describe you now? Do you want that to change? If so, how would you want to be described by others and why?
- What legacy do you want to leave? What stamp do you want to put on the world?
- What do you want to change/influence?

Finalise your personal values statement here. Aim for 150 to 200 words:

....

....

....

....

....

....

....

....

....

....

....

....

....

....

....

....

....

....

....

....

....

....

....

....

....

....

....

....

....

....

....

....

....

....

....

....

....

....

....

....

....

....

....

....

....

....

....

....

....

....

....

....

....

....

Use your personal statement to fall back on when you're faced with day-to-day decision making or those bigger life questions; it will help you to make the right decision for you.

> **TOP TIP**
> Print your statement, tell your friends and family about it, save it on your phone, write it down and put it on your walls, the bathroom mirror or wherever you will see it daily.

Personal standards

In this section we will be looking at accountability and responsibility by focusing on your personal standards. These are key principles that can be adopted along your personal journey. The concept that you are responsible for everything that happens to you and every choice that you make can be incredibly powerful when used in the right way.

The Oxford English Dictionary definition of 'accountable' is that you are responsible for something and you must explain and justify your actions. The definition of 'responsibility' is to accept that it is your duty to deal with something or take ownership of something. It is the understanding that you are the cause of what has happened and is happening. Note: you might not have directly caused something terrible to happen to you, but there is power in how you react to what's happened/happening. You can take responsibility for your response to the situation.

To put this into the context of personal development, having accountability and responsibility is understanding that you have caused either the success or failure of achieving your goals. It is also understanding that you have the power and control to influence the rest of your life: to succeed or not to succeed, whatever success looks like for you. For example, if you have set yourself a goal to spend one hour per day reading as part of your personal development, but didn't get round to it, it is being able to accept that this was your responsibility and you didn't follow your plan and therefore did not meet your goal.

Identifying as gender diverse can be incredibly hard at times for lots of different personal and societal reasons, but taking responsibility for how you respond to the world around you can help you push through these challenges and prove to yourself that you can achieve your vision of success.

> **TOP TIP**
>
> Taking responsibility for yourself and your actions means adopting a 'no excuses' approach to life.

Personal standards also refer to the way in which you want to conduct yourself and how you wish to be seen by others. It is important that you conduct yourself in line with your values, otherwise internal conflict will arise that will affect the progress towards your goals and will leave you feeling unfulfilled.

'Conduct' refers to the way in which you act and behave both in public and when people are not around. For example, ensuring your behaviour is congruent with your values even when people are not looking gives you integrity.

Some examples of behaviours or conduct traits are honesty, transparency, reliability, dedication, being supportive, treating others as you would like to be treated, being respectful and polite, honouring your commitments, remaining accountable, accepting shortcoming or mistakes, and living in line with your values.

Every person has had a time in their life when they have not conducted themselves in a way that aligns with their values and the memories of these times may be hard to reflect on. However, it is important to understand what happened so you can learn from these experiences and know what you would change in the future. It is important to be brutally honest with yourself here. Own what happened: you cannot change it, and if you do not learn from it you may end up making the same mistake again.

Consider this exercise in a positive way. When you own your failures/misconduct this can relieve the burden of having carried it around for so long and is a start towards eliminating the shame that you might feel when you remember and reflect on what happened. This is the start of your future and the start of being accountable and taking responsibility.

In this exercise, you will be reflecting upon a time when you feel you did not conduct yourself in a way that was aligned with your values. This is to enable you to identify what went wrong and what you would change in the future, and thus understand how you want to conduct yourself from now on. Be truly honest with yourself to enable you to learn as much as possible. If you are not learning, you are not moving forward, and if you are not moving forward, it becomes less likely you will achieve your goals.

Explain the situation and what happened:

....

....
....
....
....
....
....
....
....
....
....
....

Explain your behaviour and conduct at the time. What were you doing? How would you describe your actions? What were your responses? How did you conduct yourself?

....
....
....
....
....
....

What feelings does this bring up for you? How do you feel reflecting on that experience?

....
....
....
....
....
....

What do you think other people saw?

....

....
....
....
....
....

What would you do differently next time?

....
....
....
....
....
....

What are the ways in which you wished you had conducted yourself? What would your behaviour look like if you had another chance to re-live this moment in your life?

....
....
....
....
....
....

What is important to you in relation to your conduct? What do you want people to say about you when you are not there to hear it? This is designed to help you reflect on the exercise to gain a new perspective on the situation as opposed to placing value on what others think of you.

....
....
....
....
....
....

A personal Code of Conduct can help you to remain accountable and responsible for your behaviours and actions. Considering all the above in relation to how you want to conduct yourself, make three personal commitments here. This is your Code of Conduct:

I commit/promise to...

I commit/promise to...

I commit/promise to...

Now you have understood your core values and how you want to conduct yourself when navigating your life, it is up to you to put this into practice in the future. Take every opportunity to examine your conduct: are you really practising your life in the ways in which you committed to above? If not, take responsibility for what has happened, learn from your experiences and try again.

> **TOP TIP**
>
> You can use this exercise to examine your behaviour and conduct in the future when you feel you could have acted or responded differently. Use this as an opportunity to develop and not a way in which to constantly criticise yourself.

SNAPSHOT

- Put your values at the heart of every decision that you make. Practise this daily, making a conscious effort to make choices aligned with your values. Practise with smaller decisions first. For example, if one of your personal values is health, are you making the right choice for lunch?
- Print out/write out your personal Code of Conduct and put it somewhere that you will see it every single day. This could be on the bathroom mirror or even the front door. This will serve as a daily reminder to help you conduct yourself in line with the standards you have set. It will soon become second nature and a part of who you are.
- Your values may change over time. Use the values exercises to review them at key points in your life. This could be after a significant life event or after a certain amount of time has passed.
  - ➡ Do not forget to review your personal standards and Code of Conduct as well – these may change as your values change.

📷 If you feel conflicted about something that's happened in your life and feel that you could have done something differently, use the exercises in the personal standards section above to examine your behaviour, review what you could have done differently and use this to learn and move forward.

Learning styles

As we will touch upon in the chapter on values, it is important that you understand yourself so you can build a strong foundation to start setting your goals and achieving your preferred future. One way in which you can start to understand how you operate as a person is by finding out more about the way in which you learn. There are many different learning styles; here we'll focus on four learning styles within one model and the underlying principles of how learning occurs.

Kolb's learning theory

David Kolb introduced his theory of learning in 1984.[1] The theory is a multi-faceted approach utilising two distinct levels to understanding how people learn. The first level identifies a four-stage learning process: the process you must go through to embed learning. The second level is an understanding of how you learn and which way you learn best.

Kolb's cycle of learning is represented here:

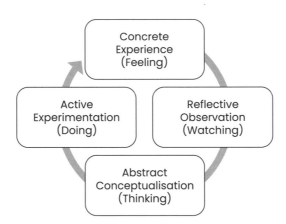

1. **Concrete Experience** (Feeling): We experience a new encounter/situation.
2. **Reflective Observation** (Watching): We reflect on the new encounter/situation; we consider if there are any new experiences or differences between experience and understanding.

---

1   See www.simplypsychology.org/learning-kolb.htm

3. **Abstract Conceptualisation** (Thinking): We start to understand the situation/encounter as a new idea/concept.
4. **Active Experimentation** (Doing): We put the new idea/concept into practice, applying it to real-life situations to see what happens.

At each stage of the learning process, Kolb identifies that we experience the cycle through four different ways of learning: either by feeling, watching, thinking or doing. Kolb theorises that our learning style is a combination of two elements of the models but that each pair operates on a single axis and therefore some elements cannot operate together. For example, we cannot think and feel as part of the learning process but can think and watch or feel and do. This is shown in the following table:

	Active Experimentation (Doing)	Reflective Observation (Watching)
Concrete Experience (Feeling)	Accommodating	Diverging
Abstract Conceptualisation (Thinking)	Converging	Assimilating

By using this table and understanding how you experience the learning process by either feeling, watching, thinking or doing, you can then understand your learning style. As shown in the table, Kolb identifies the following as learning styles:

1. **Accommodating** – a combination of doing and feeling. It is a 'hands on' approach to learning through experiences.
2. **Diverging** – a combination of feeling and watching. This is preferring to watch rather than do.
3. **Converging** – a combination of doing and thinking. This is having the ability to utilise theory and put this into practice.
4. **Assimilating** – a combination of watching and thinking. It is generally using a practical and logical approach to concepts.

It is important you understand the process of learning and then work out which style represents the way you learn. When you start to set your goals and create the process through which you will achieve them, this should be congruent with your learning style. This will make reaching your targets easier.

There are many quizzes you can take online to understand your learning style. Search for Kolb's learning style questionnaire, take a quiz and make a note of your learning style here:

....

....

As you work through this book and write your goals, it is important that you refer to this section to reflect on whether the strategies you put in place for achieving them is a good fit with your learning style. By having strategies and processes that reflect your learning style, you'll be able to learn new things a lot easier and achieve your goals a lot quicker. If your strategies are not reflective of how you learn, you can become frustrated and demotivated, and therefore struggle to reach your full potential.

Chapter 2

Goal-Setting Models and Principles

Goal-setting models and theories have been used for years to support people with everything from personal development to business development, health, fitness and wellbeing, and even to gain financial control. Goal-setting theories, models and principles are more popular than ever because when people start to put these principles into practice, they realise that they work. Once people put in some time to get to know what works for them, they increase their productivity, learn new skills, adapt and reach goals they had never thought were possible.

This chapter will give you the underpinning foundations and principles you'll need to write your goals, understand your preferred future and reach new life possibilities that you thought were only imaginable.

There are many goal-setting models and theories. We'll focus on a few to give an understanding of each so you can choose what works best for you. It's important that you're able to recognise what models and strategies suit your learning style as this will give you a stronger foundation for success and keep you motivated to achieve your goals.

It is important to understand the underpinning concepts of setting and writing goals and how these can impact on success. Goal-setting models will help you to improve and maintain your motivation and drive, giving you a clear focus for each step in your plan and how this links to your overall plan. These models will give you more direction when working towards your goals, as well as a sense of purpose and achievement when you reach them. Using goal-setting models will also help you to make the most of your time and resources, and therefore your life! Effective planning is the key to success for any project, including personal development.

As I explained in the section about personal values in the previous chapter, it's important that any goals you set and what you do to reach them are aligned with your personal values. This ensures that you are living your life in alignment with what's important to you, leading ultimately to a feeling of fulfilment.

As you learn and develop, your goals might change, and you will start to see what you are capable of. You might start to consider achieving things that you thought were only possible for others. You can use the goal-setting models throughout all areas of your life to achieve any goal that you set for yourself, no matter how big or small.

Your goals and the process of achieving them should be considered as a journey. You will learn a lot about yourself through engaging in the process rather than focusing solely on achieving the outcome. Try to stay in the moment as you work through this process. Time is not guaranteed, life is not guaranteed, so it is important that you are not working towards a goal that does not excite and interest you. You cannot guarantee that tomorrow will happen; the only guarantee of time we have is the moment right now.

In the short term you may have to carry out tasks that you don't particularly enjoy to reach your goal; however, it is important that you get the balance right so that you enjoy the process too.

That is not to say that there's no point working towards a three-, six- or twelve-month goal to create your preferred future; it's just important that you realise that you shouldn't wait to reach your goal to be happy; the process should be enjoyable and worth the outcome.

According to *Forbes Magazine* (2020)[1] the most successful people are those that dream big, write it down and focus on the process rather than the outcome.

In this chapter, we will examine these models:

+ the GROW model of goal setting
+ SMART criteria
+ the gamer's approach
+ Locke and Latham's goal-setting theory, and
+ the endowment effect.

It is important that you understand these models as they will be used throughout this book in different activities.

Let's start by assessing where you're currently at. Do this by using the star model below to 'measure' each area on a scale of 1 to 6. 1 means you are not happy with this area, and it needs significant improvement; 6 means you are completely fulfilled in this area and do not feel any further progress needs to be made.

---

1 https://www.forbes.com/sites/carolinecastrillon/2020/03/15/this-is-how-highly-successful-people-achieve-career-goals/?sh=682d92d178dd

Where are you now?

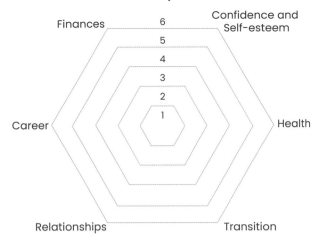

Mark where you are on each section with a cross. Connect the crosses with a single line. This will help you see how much things have improved or changed when we complete another assessment in the future to review your progress.

Which areas need the most improvement? Write them in order of importance in relation to which needs the most work first (1 being the lowest score and therefore requiring the most work, 6 being the highest score, requiring the least work):

1. ....

2. ....

3. ....

4. ....

5. ....

6. ....

You can skip to the chapters in the order that you have written them above and work through the book in this way. For example, if you have identified confidence and self-esteem as needing the most improvement, go to this chapter of the book first and work through it. By starting with the most challenging areas, you will find the other areas a lot easier to tackle because you'll have built a stronger foundation for yourself and will be less likely to give up. Before you begin this, finish reading this chapter first to support you when working through the other chapters.

GROW model

The GROW model of goal setting has become one of the most popular and success-ful models used for self-improvement, personal development and performance improvement worldwide. Developed by Sir John Whitmore in the 1980s, it helps to unlock potential as well as improving confidence and motivation. It does this by using a *solution-focused* approach to reaching goals. The GROW model supports its users to think about their current situation, identify their preferred future and then provide a framework to bridge the gap between the two states.

Here are the underlying principles:

G – Goals/aspirations
R – Reality (current situation)
O – Options/opportunities
W – Will

Let's look at what the model means in context for you.

Goals/aspirations

+ What do you want to achieve?
+ What is the goal?
+ When will you achieve your goal?
+ What are the benefits for you if you achieve your goal?
+ Will anyone else benefit by you completing this goal?

Reality

+ What is the current situation?
+ Have you made any steps towards your goal already?
+ Are there any barriers that you are currently facing to achieving your goal?
+ What resources do you currently have that will help you?
+ What do you know about yourself already that will help you achieve your goal?

Options/opportunities

+ What are your options in relation to achieving your goal?
+ Can you identify any opportunities that will help you achieve your goal?
+ Is there anyone that can help you with identifying an option/opportunity?
+ What are the benefits and drawbacks of each of your options/opportunities?
+ What else can you do?

Will

+ How committed are you to achieving your goals?
+ Which options/opportunities will you choose to act on first?
+ When will you start taking action?
+ Scale your commitment – how committed are you on a scale of 1 to 10, 1 being not committed, 10 being fully committed?
+ If it's not a 10, what can you do to make it a 10 or even to move it just one point towards a 10?
+ What will happen if you do not act? What will happen if you do act?

These questions will help you to understand each section of the model and support you to move forward with achieving your goals. You can revisit these questions at any point throughout your life with any goal that you have identified.

The questions are examples and you do not have to answer all of them in order – they are merely a guide to help you with setting and achieving your goals by ensuring you have thought through your goal, it is achievable and you want what you have planned for. Do not choose a goal because you feel it is what society or others expect you to achieve, for example a big house, a fast car, loads of cash in the bank. If that is not what you genuinely want, you will not find that ultimate fulfilment; you will have fulfilled someone else's dreams. Make sure you check in with yourself when you are writing your goals to ensure they align with your core values, tuning in to the prospect of how they make you feel. If you're not looking forward to your next steps, your preferred future, and the idea that you'll achieve it, then I'd urge you to think again about the goal you have set for yourself. Your goals should always align with your core values – they should interest and excite you into wanting to get started straight away! If they don't, the process will be more challenging to achieve. Remember, enjoying the journey will help give you a sense of satisfaction and will motivate you along the way.

> **TOP TIP**
> You'll either work hard to create your dream or you'll work hard to create someone else's.

The SMART criteria

As we touched upon earlier, we also need to understand the SMART criteria. The SMART tool is excellent to use when you're writing your more specific goals because it ensures that they are realistic and that you are not setting yourself up to fail. Therefore, your motivation and drive to achieve your goal will remain even when the unexpected might happen in your life, because the plan is still realistic and achievable. The SMART acronym is used throughout this book so before you move on to other chapters, make sure you have a strong understand of how the tool works so you can put it into practice:

S – Specific
M – Measurable
A – Achievable
R – Realistic
T – Timely

Each of the elements on their own are useful and important, and even if you only use one of the elements to write your goals you will still gain some positive benefits. However, when you put them all together and use them collectively, you'll super charge your progress and your goals will become a reality. Let's look at each of the acronyms in more detail. For this example, we'll use writing your first book.

Specific

Is your goal specific enough? Is it targeted enough? Or is it too broad? Under the SMART criteria you need to ensure that your goal is **specific**.

Using the example of writing your first book, your initial goal could be 'to write a book'. To make this more **specific** you need to narrow it down further. Your initial goal could then look like 'to write a romance novel'. Adding additional details makes this more specific, if you know what you're aiming for in as much detail as possible then you have a benchmark for success.

Measurable

How will you know when you have completed your goal? Is it **measurable**? In the example above, if you write your goal as 'to write a romance novel', then once you've written 200 words, have you therefore achieved your goal? Or are you looking to write more words so that it becomes a book as opposed to just a paragraph?

To make your goal more measurable, you can include a word count. Your goal could look like: 'to write a 60,000-word romance novel'. This gives you an idea of how many words you'd need to write to achieve your goal of writing your own book. You'll know when you've achieved your goal because you have a target to aim for of 60,000 words and therefore have something to measure your goal against. You can track your progress each week by calculating how many words you have written and this will give you the opportunity to assess whether you will meet your goal.

Achievable

It's important that whilst you should dream big and make sure you're aiming for the stars, your goal is still **achievable**. It doesn't matter how big your dream or goal might be, if the steps to getting there are achievable then you'll achieve your goal. We've talked previously about the small steps approach to goal setting and planning and this section starts to draw upon those principles. You might want to write a comic or a textbook, both of which are achievable; however, are they achievable in a short space of time? Are they achievable in your current circumstances utilising the resources that you have? Do you have access to the resources you need to achieve this goal? For example, if you have access to a laptop, time, the knowledge, the creativity and tools to write either a comic or a textbook then you might achieve your goal of writing a book in a shorter space of time than someone who has other competing priorities. Your goal of writing a book wouldn't be achievable if it was to write a textbook in a week. So, ensuring that you think about what is achievable and what you want to do, is a crucial component of the goal setting process. Your goal might look like this: 'to write a 60,000-word romance novel in one year'. This means you'd have to write 1155 words per week. If that's achievable to you given other things going on in your life then great; if not, scale it back again to make it achievable to you.

Realistic

Building on the achievable section, **realistic** and achievable go hand in hand. You need to ensure that at the same time as shooting for the stars you are being realistic, otherwise you'll end up de-motivated and chasing something that is potentially unattainable. This doesn't mean that you shouldn't think big or try in the first place. You just need to ensure that what you are aiming for is reasonable, that it stretches and challenges you but is still realistic. In relation to the example of writing a book, if your goal is to write a book in a week and have it published the next week, this isn't realistic. But to consider your goal as 'to write a 60,000-word romantic novel', it makes it much more realistic to achieve. Writing a book is a big undertaking, but with small steps and strategic approach, writing your first book can become a reality.

Timely

In the examples above, we talked about the unrealistic and unachievable goal of writing a book in a week and having it published the next week because this isn't timely and by not being timely therefore the goal is unrealistic.

Back to the writing a book example: this should include a timeframe and one that is realistic and timely. To write a 60,000-word romantic novel in one year gives you a timeframe to work towards and helps you break down the goal into even smaller steps. To write a 60,000-word romantic novel in one year by writing 1155 words per week makes it achievable, realistic and timely. Writing a book is an impressive achievement but when you break the goal down into writing 1155 words per week, it's much less impressive but very SMART and therefore attainable. When writing your goals, consider breaking them down into three or four smaller goals, all of which should be SMART and should feed into your overall goal. If your goal is to write a 60,000-word romantic novel in one year, work backwards from that to make smaller, achievable, realistic goals that will keep you motivated. This might even include factoring in SMART goals to develop characters, storylines and research publishers.

Taking into consideration all that we have learnt now in relation to the SMART acronym your new goal might look something like this:

> to write a 60,000-word romantic novel in one year by writing 1155 words per week.

We broke down the writing a book goal into manageable smaller goals by introducing a weekly/daily goal, now we need to make these goals even smaller. To do this we need to consider the process that we will take to achieve the 1155 words per week. This should consist of the completion of daily tasks to reach your weekly goal. Your daily goals should align themselves with your weekly goal. Your daily goals could look like this:

> to write 165 words per day between 10am and 11:30am.

Your daily goal should also be SMART.

To write 165 words per day at 4am every day for one hour might not be realistic or achievable if you're not used to getting up at 4am every day. Ensuring that writing works around your current lifestyle and building time into your day to focus on writing a very small amount makes your sub goals SMART. If you don't feel that writing 165 words per day is achievable, then make your overall goal longer and work backwards to scale back your daily goal to something more manageable that's a smaller sub goal which is SMART and feeds into your overall goal. The goal is small, simple, specific, straightforward and easy to follow. The emphasis should always be on achieving the next smallest step rather than focusing on the bigger picture and the overall goal. The thought of writing 60,000 words in a year might be overwhelming and daunting but writing 165 words per day and implementing your sub goals and smaller steps is much more achievable and realistic. You should always focus on achieving the next smallest step because if you don't achieve it, you will struggle to achieve the overall goal. Remember, writing a book is just an example, but the principles apply to any goal you want to set in any area of your life.

The gamer's approach

To help you understand the small steps approach to goal setting, think of it as if you're playing a game on a games console. The aim of the game is to complete each level, and the levels get harder each time as you move through them. If you're working on completing a game, you don't think about the bigger final level; all your focus and attention is on achieving the level you are on. To complete the level you're working on you might have to try multiple times, and each time you'll change your strategy for doing so ever so slightly based on learning from your experiences of playing the game. This will then help you to try again, try something different and, eventually, through smaller steps of changing strategy and continuous attempts you'll finally complete the level. Once you've done this you will have the time and headspace to focus on the next level – the aim being the grand finale and completion of the game (the goal). You can't skip to the final level of the game without going through the levels to get there, learning and developing your strategy as you move through the game.

To put that into context, by moving through each of the smaller daily tasks/goals you will learn about what strategies work, what mindset you need to be in and what attitude works for you. You'll fine tune all this over time to achieve your bigger and future goals. So, if you get stuck on a level in your game and you ask your friend to complete it for you, they get you through to the harder level, but how do you expect to be able to achieve the harder level if you didn't complete the previous one? The same is true of your goals: if you miss out a step, try to rush to the end or make goals whereby the steps are too big (not SMART), you're more likely not to achieve your goal. You won't have had the chance to learn, develop and hone your skills, enabling you to reach higher levels of success and therefore reach your goal. This also means that you will only ever achieve a finite amount of success if you're not willing to go through the process of learning, taking smaller steps and achieving bigger goals over time.

> **TOP TIP**
> We are the product of the choices that we make every single day.

When embarking on any personal development mission, significant and long-term sustainable change takes hard work, small steps, dedication and perseverance – alongside good goal setting! No one can achieve your goals and dreams for you, so it's time to dig deep, take yourself seriously and show yourself what you're capable of achieving. Being gender diverse comes with its own challenges. It can be tough at times but if you've already taken steps towards transitioning and coming out, you'll be able to transfer those skills to your personal development goals. Coming out and transitioning take perseverance, patience and courage, so you've already got those to draw upon.

Locke and Latham's goal-setting theory and five principles of goal setting

Locke and Latham developed their goal-setting theory based on the evidence of over 400 studies.[2] There are many benefits to using Locke and Latham's goal-setting theory. It can help to set a course, establish a commitment, drive planning, analyse and solve problems as well as giving you the opportunity to practise perseverance and overcome obstacles. Practising perseverance and overcoming obstacles is a key skill to develop; it's easy to throw in the towel when problems occur and to give up when things get a bit tough. One of the most important factors when working to achieve your goals is your ability to problem solve, overcome obstacles and find creative ways forward. This takes practice and drive and ultimately comes down to how badly you want to achieve your goal.

Locke's theory is that people are much more likely to achieve their goals if they are specific and measurable rather than general: for example, 'to eat healthier' vs 'to eat breakfast every day'. 'To eat healthier' is not as specific as 'to eat breakfast every day'. Locke also identified that it was important for the goals to be challenging without being impossible. A goal that is too easy to reach won't motivate you to continue your journey and a goal that is too difficult will demotivate you easily and you're more likely to fail.

Locke and Latham identified five principles of effective goal setting:

- **Clarify** – The goal should be specific and clear, so you know exactly what you're aiming for.
- **Challenging** – Pick a goal that you're not sure you can achieve, but you know isn't impossible.

---

2   www.nationalforum.com/Electronic%20Journal%20Volumes/Lunenburg,%20Fred%20
      C.%20Goal-Setting%20Theoryof%20Motivation%20IJMBA%20V15%20N1%202011.pdf

✦ **Commitment** – Make sure you hold yourself accountable; the only way you'll achieve your goal is if you are committed to taking action.

✦ **Feedback** – Analyse your progress and consider what went well and what can be improved. You can use an accountability buddy to help you, especially if you and your buddy are trying to achieve your own set of goals. Give constructive feedback to each other.

✦ **Task complexity** – This is the planning stage, the small steps part whereby you'll break down the goal into smaller sub-goals, reviewing your plan and progress at key intervals.

As you can see, there are a lot of different goal-setting principles and theories that have similarities and whose foundations have a substantial evidence base.

> **TOP TIP**
>
> If you keep doing what you've always done, you'll always get what you've always got.

The endowment effect

The endowment effect is the concept that if we own something, we don't like to give it up so easily.[3] Daniel Kahneman and colleagues developed the endowment effect by giving half a group of students mugs and asking the students to sell them; the other half of the group were buyers.[4] The sellers had to set a price that they would be willing to sell their mug for and the buyers identified how much they would be willing to buy a mug for. The results showed that the sellers wanted significantly more money for their mugs than the buyers were willing to pay for them because their attachment was greater.

When we put this into the context of goal setting, we understand that if we 'own' our goals, we are less likely to give up and to let things get in our way of achieving them. Activities such as visualisation can help us own our future achievements. Visualisation is an important skill that can be used in lots of different ways. Have a go at visualising your preferred future now. For five minutes, visualise yourself achieving your goal and try to imagine what this feels like, who is there, where you are and what you have overcome to get there.

---

3 For an overview see www.sciencedirect.com/topics/medicine-and-dentistry/endowment-effect#: ~:text=279).,(1990%2C%201991

4 Kahneman, D., Knetsch, J.L. and Thaler, R.H. (1990) 'Experimental Tests of the Endowment Effect and the Coase Theorem.' *Journal of Political Economy 98*, 6, 1325–1348.

Now you've completed this exercise, answer the following questions and share your reflections in the space below:

- ✦ What does achieving your goal look like for you?
- ✦ How do you feel once you've achieved your goal?
- ✦ How has achieving your goal changed your life?
- ✦ What have you gained from achieving your goal?
- ✦ What have you learnt about yourself from achieving your goal?

....

....

....

....

....

....

....

....

....

....

....

....

....

....

....

....

....

....

....

....

....

....

....

....

....

....

....

....

....

....

....

....

....

....

....

....

....

Setting your own goals

It's time to start looking at setting your own personalised goals. We'll look at how you can implement all that you have learnt and start you off on your path to success!

Now you understand the core principles of goal-setting theory, we can bring these together to form a simple strategy that you'll implement throughout the rest of this book. This process was first developed in the 1950s by Doctor William Deming, initially to understand why processes within his sector didn't work and how it could learn from what happened to move forward and reach its preferred outcome. His approach has been adopted for use within a variety of sectors, including within coaching, to help encourage productivity, produce effective results and support people to move towards their preferred futures.[5]

The strategy, like others, has four main elements:

1. Identify.
2. Plan.
3. Execute.
4. Review.

---

5   See www.mindtools.com/pages/article/newPPM_89.htm

We'll use this strategy as the foundation for working through the different chapters of the book. This will help you to **identify** your goals, **plan** how you'll reach them, **execute** your plan and **review** your progress – learning from your reviews and making small tweaks to your plans to propel you forward towards your overall goal.

There are many different types of goals that you can work on. Here are some categories to consider to get you started (this list is not exhaustive, so if there's something you want to work on that doesn't appear here, you can still use this book to work through that):

- Transition and identity.
- Home and family.
- Financial, business and career.
- Health, fitness/physical goals.
- Attitude and social life.
- Leisure.
- Community/contributing to society.
- Spiritual goals.
- Education.

One of the key things to remember when embarking upon this journey is that writing goals and working towards them go hand in hand. You will not achieve your goals by writing a goal – you must put in the work to achieve what you're aiming for; no one is going to hand it to you on a plate.

SNAPSHOT

- Using the GROW model to understand goal-setting models generally can help to give you the foundations for success. Without understanding key models like this it will be harder to write your goals, and it will be more difficult for you to achieve your goals – give yourself the best chance of success!
- Utilise the SMART criteria for when you write your goals. This will ensure that you are much more likely to achieve what you are setting out to. Ensuring goals are SMART is a recipe for success!
- Locke and Latham's five principles for goal setting will support you along your journey and you can use the models interchangeably and even for different goals.
- Use the model that you think suits you best, otherwise you'll compromise your enjoyment of the process.

- 📷 Own your goals, own your future. Visualise your preferred future and goals whenever and wherever possible to ensure that you're owning it – and therefore less likely to give up.
- 📷 It's the small steps that lead to victory!

• Chapter 3 •

Self-Esteem and Confidence

Self-esteem

Self-esteem is someone's overall sense of their personal worth; it is one of the most important things you can possess and value in life. Having higher levels of self-esteem can lead to better overall health, general wellbeing and a sense of fulfilment and belonging. Self-esteem as a gender diverse person can be difficult to come by, especially with all the stories you hear in the media about trans identities, the discrimination that you might have experienced yourself and the general lack of understanding from others about what it means to be trans. Gender diverse people can experience crippling levels of anxiety and extremely low levels of self-esteem because of the impact of dysphoria, for example. Society's perceptions of trans and gender diverse people in general can at times be incredibly hostile, which can also contribute to low self-esteem. It is also important to recognise, however, that there are many allies for gender diverse communities, and awareness of trans issues is building and services are becoming more inclusive.

Self-esteem is important because this can influence the choices that you make every day, and as discussed in previous chapters, the actions you take daily will decide whether you achieve your goals. Higher levels of self-esteem are associated with making positive choices, because you are more likely to be concerned about the potential impact on yourself based on the decision you're making. Lower levels of self-esteem are associated with more destructive choices, and those with lower self-esteem can appear to not care about the consequences of their choices. People with higher levels of self-esteem can be more motivated to take care of themselves and strive to reach their personal goals and achievements. However, those with lower self-esteem can struggle to take care of their basic needs because they don't feel worthy of happiness and fulfilment or don't believe they can achieve more than they already are. Low self-esteem has a significant impact on whether someone achieves their personal development/career/health goals. Those with lower

43

levels of self-esteem may also struggle to overcome barriers that are put in the way of them achieving their goals because once those barriers present themselves, people are more likely to tell themselves they can't move forward or that 'it wasn't meant to be'. Self-esteem is crucial to overall wellbeing and you can optimise your self-esteem to help you achieve your goals.

Gender diverse people can struggle with lower levels of self-esteem because of the impact of gender dysphoria, transition issues, discrimination, family rejection, bullying and mental health issues. In a study conducted by Cornell University, transitioning is associated with higher levels of self-esteem as people find more acceptance of their bodies and how they present themselves to the world.[1] This can also give people higher levels of confidence. This study identifies that gender affirmation surgery and social transition suggest that gender diverse people can reach their full potential if they are living their lives in accordance with their gender identity.

Low self-esteem can have a significant impact on overall wellbeing. It can cause issues such as anxiety, stress, loneliness and depression, as well as issues within relationships and friendships and decreased performance/productivity at school, college or work. Self-esteem can therefore have far-reaching consequences on many different areas of your life and needs to be treated as a fundamental pillar of your existence.

Preferred futures

We've discussed preferred futures a couple of times already. Simply put, it means asking yourself what you want your future to look like. It's an opportunity to visualise what you want your life to be like in the future, what you see yourself doing and what you envision you will have achieved. An opportunity to dream without limitations is an opportunity to take a step towards your preferred future.

Thinking about self-esteem, what would your preferred future look like? Visualise it. If you had higher levels of self-esteem, what would you be like? What would you look like? How would you feel? Write down your thoughts here:

....

....

....

....

---

1   https://whatweknow.inequality.cornell.edu/topics/lgbt-equality/what-does-the-scholarly
     -research-say-about-the-well-being-of-transgender-people

....

....

In this section we'll start to work towards the preferred future you've identified above. We'll work through a process to help you understand where your self-esteem is now and identify SMART goals to help achieve your vision.

> **TOP TIP**
>
> Visualisation is an important tool to have; use it to visualise your preferred future as much as possible!

Rosenberg's Self-Esteem scale

Let's start by looking at where your self-esteem is currently. You might feel confident that you've got high or low self-esteem, or you might be surprised by what you find. Be sure to be honest with yourself in this self-assessment because if you aren't, you are doing yourself a disservice. If you are not honest at this stage, you might start on a journey that is a little off-kilter, leading you down a path that might not be right for you.

For this exercise we'll use Rosenberg's Self-Esteem scale (RSE).[2] The RSE consists of ten statements to measure global self-esteem related to overall feelings of self-worth or self-acceptance.[3]

Below is a list of statements. Identify how strongly you agree/disagree with each of the statements in relation to your general feelings about yourself:

1. Overall, I am satisfied with myself.
   a. Strongly agree
   b. Agree
   c. Disagree
   d. Strongly disagree
2. At times I think I am no good at all.
   a. Strongly agree
   b. Agree
   c. Disagree
   d. Strongly disagree

---

2   M. Rosenberg (1965) *Society and the Adolescent Self-Image*. Princeton, NJ: Princeton University Press.

3   https://exploringyourmind.com/the-rosenberg-self-esteem-scale

3. I feel I have several good qualities.
    a. Strongly agree
    b. Agree
    c. Disagree
    d. Strongly disagree
4. I can do things as well as most other people.
    a. Strongly agree
    b. Agree
    c. Disagree
    d. Strongly disagree
5. I feel I do not have much to be proud of.
    a. Strongly agree
    b. Agree
    c. Disagree
    d. Strongly disagree
6. I certainly feel useless at times.
    a. Strongly agree
    b. Agree
    c. Disagree
    d. Strongly disagree
7. I feel that I'm a person of worth, at least on an equal plane with others.
    a. Strongly agree
    b. Agree
    c. Disagree
    d. Strongly disagree
8. I wish I could have more respect for myself.
    a. Strongly agree
    b. Agree
    c. Disagree
    d. Strongly disagree
9. All in all, I am inclined to feel that I am a failure.
    a. Strongly agree
    b. Agree
    c. Disagree
    d. Strongly disagree
10. I take a positive attitude towards myself.
    a. Strongly agree
    b. Agree
    c. Disagree
    d. Strongly disagree

To find out your score, apply the following points to each of the questions:

For questions 1, 2, 4, 6 and 7:
Strongly agree = 3
Agree = 2
Disagree = 1
Strongly disagree = 0

And for questions 3, 5, 8, 9 and 10, apply the following points:

Strongly agree = 0
Agree = 1
Disagree = 2
Strongly disagree = 3

Add up your points for all the questions and write the total here: ....

The scale ranges from 0 to 30. Scores between 15 and 25 are categorised as being within a normal self-esteem range. Some improvements would be beneficial; however, they are not necessarily required for healthy functioning.

Scores below 15 identify low self-esteem and therefore it is crucial that some improvements are made to support healthier functioning and increased likelihood of reaching your full potential.

Limiting beliefs

Often having lower levels of self-esteem comes with its own set of limiting beliefs. Limiting beliefs are the messages you tell yourself on a regular basis that prevent you reaching your full potential. They are messages that *limit* what you believe you can do, and they are incredibly powerful in shaping your identity and your future. The more often you tell yourself what your limits are, the more likely you are to believe them. By becoming aware of your limiting beliefs you can change them and start to send yourself some stronger messages that don't limit your potential and help you on your way towards your preferred future.

To try to conquer your limiting beliefs you first need to know what they are. It is important to understand what your limiting beliefs are and that you change them at the source rather than treating the symptoms.

You've reflected on your preferred future already. Now ask yourself the following questions to establish what your limiting beliefs are. Use this as an opportunity to reflect on your thought process and internal dialogue.

✦ Why haven't you achieved your preferred future yet?

✦ What is holding you back?

✦ What are you telling yourself to prevent you from trying or starting to work towards your preferred future?

✦ Is there anything specific that you tell yourself that is holding you back? For example, 'I'm not good enough, no one would want what I offer', and so on.

✦ If you had to describe yourself to other people, what would you leave out or include that constitutes a limiting belief?

✦ What are the common messages you've heard from others throughout your life that you have started to believe?

Note your findings here:

....

....

....

....

....

....

....

....

....

....

....

....

Of the above, are there one or two limiting beliefs that you feel are significantly holding you back over the others? Write them here:

....

....

....

....

Where do you think these limiting beliefs have come from? Has anyone said them to you? Are they from your childhood? Your experiences?

....

....

....

....

....

....

If you're unsure about where your limiting beliefs come from, don't worry; it's not crucial to understand where they come from but can help to put them into context for you. This in turn can help you understand why those limiting beliefs are not true and how they have held you back for so long.

If you've identified that your limiting beliefs have come from other people, this will only have power if you give it power. Other people's negative or destructive opinions of you reflect them and not you. You can choose to believe what others believe, or you can choose to trust yourself and your potential. The relationships chapter will help you devise strategies to help manage this.

It's important that you understand what skills and qualities you do have that will help you move towards your preferred future instead of focusing on your limiting beliefs. Knowing your limiting beliefs helps to remember that they are only that. The more aware you are of this, the easier it will be to put those beliefs aside and focus on the skills you have that will help you achieve your goals. Let's think about your previous experiences.

Think about a time when you achieved something that was important to you. Your achievement can be anything from a big life event to a day-to-day task. What was it?

....

....

....

....

How did you manage to achieve it? Did you have any strategies? How did you move from point A to point B? What did you need to learn/develop/consider that helped you along the way?

....

....

....

....

....

....

How did you feel once you had achieved what you set out to?

....

....

....

....

Looking back on your achievement, what skills and qualities do you think were required for you to achieve your goal? Here are some strengths to help you in your reflections:

Determination	Drive	Commitment	Perseverance	Dedication
Passion	Focus	Patience	Self-belief	Doggedness
Courage	Energy	Strength	Resilience	Discipline

....

....

....

....

....

If there are other strengths not listed above, still write them down. These are more important than the suggestions!

If you've struggled to complete this section, ask someone that you trust the above questions and write down what they think. Other people's perceptions of us can be quite different and much more positive than what we think about ourselves.

Of the above strengths, which do you think are the most important qualities that helped you to achieve your goal? Which strengths do you think will help you most in reaching your preferred future? Write them below as statements that apply to you, starting with 'I am...' or 'I have...':

1. ....

2. ....

3. ....

These are your personal strengths; these are what make you different to everyone else, and they are the strengths that will help you realise your full potential.

It can take years to improve self-esteem and confidence and these strategies can be a starting point. Just completing this exercise in isolation or to work through this section of the book will not give you higher levels of self-esteem alone; implementing strategies will support you through this process.

People reach their preferred futures by making choices every day that fall in line with their vision and values, and the choices that you make are reflective of how you feel about yourself. If self-esteem is something you need to work on, then consider what your goals for your self-esteem will be.

> **TOP TIP**
> Being aware of your limiting beliefs will help you overcome them and become a better, limitless version of yourself.

Writing self-esteem goals

Writing self-esteem goals can be tricky, but there's plenty here to help you. For many gender diverse people, self-esteem can be linked to the perceptions we have about ourselves in relation to gender and how we present ourselves to the world. This is often linked to the concept of 'passing', and people's self-esteem can be affected daily if they feel they do not pass or are being misgendered whilst out in the world. This can affect mental health and emotional wellbeing and can slowly chip away at any self-esteem you do have, leaving you feeling low and not very hopeful about the future.

Self-esteem goals in this area can be related to trying out new things to help you feel better about your gender identity. For example, have you been meaning to try out some new clothes? A new look? Even things like binding, packing or tucking? You can write your self-esteem goals around things like this too. The point of setting goals around image is not to make you feel you must 'pass' more; it's about making you feel good about yourself and not conforming to other people's standards of image in relation to binary gender identities.

It might be that you've been 'out' as a trans person for a long time and want to improve your self-esteem by taking steps towards believing in yourself and reaching bigger career goals. Or it might be that you're just starting your transition and want to improve your self-esteem by participating in acts that affirm your gender. Keep in mind that whatever your goals, they must be SMART and incorporate a small steps approach.

> **TOP TIP**
> Don't limit yourself to other people's perceptions of image, 'passing' or identity; focus on yourself and how you want to feel!

Strategies for improving self-esteem

There are many practical strategies you can use to help improve your self-esteem. In this section we'll explore what works best for you and this will help you to write more specific self-esteem goals. You don't have to incorporate all the strategies below into your day-to-day life, but you can work through them to help you find out what works best for you. Even if you complete an activity that you think might not work for you, you'll still learn something about yourself – you'll learn what doesn't feel right! Try them all, pick the ones that work best and work these into the goals you'll set yourself later in the chapter.

Positive affirmations

Affirmations can be incredibly powerful. An affirmation is a statement or proposition that is declared to be true, and when you say these to yourself, based on what you have written, you can use them to *affirm* beliefs in yourself. This helps you to start to believe the statements you've written and if they are based on reaching your preferred future, will help you get there. For positive affirmations to be useful, consistency is the key – you'll need to commit to hearing your affirmations and hearing them regularly. Don't expect to tell yourself an affirmation once and start to believe it; like all aspects of personal development this takes time, consistency and effort. Some examples of positive affirmations are as follows:

- ✦ I know, accept and am true to myself.
- ✦ I believe in, trust and have confidence in myself.
- ✦ I know I can accomplish anything I set my mind to.
- ✦ I believe in me.
- ✦ I am proud of myself and all that I have achieved.
- ✦ I deserve love, compassion and empathy.
- ✦ I matter. I am allowed to say 'no' to others and 'yes' to myself.

Thinking about your preferred future and what you want to achieve in relation to improving your self-esteem, reflect on your limiting beliefs – what positive affirmations can you write for yourself that will support you to move towards your preferred future and away from your limiting beliefs? Make sure you write them in the present tense. They should be short, specific and positive. Remember – these should be personal to you. Don't write affirmations that you think you should have; write them based on what you want or need to hear.

Identify them here:

1. ....
2. ....
3. ....

If using positive affirmations is going to work for you, there are ways in which you can implement this into your daily life. Here are some tips to help you figure out how you can build these into your daily routine:

- Write your affirmations on sticky notes and put them around your house in places that you will see them. Note that you must be able to read them and not just see them. It is reading and believing your affirmations that will help support you on your journey.
- Write them on a piece of paper and stick them on the front door. Before you leave the house for the day, take a moment to read each one twice, focusing only on absorbing the words.
- Set a background on your laptop/phone/devices that has your affirmations on it. Whenever you use your devices, make time to focus in on these. If you use your phone to do this, you can spend a couple of minutes a day in your breaks, travel time or whilst you make a cup of tea even, reading your affirmations and taking in their meaning.
- When you wake up in the morning, repeat your affirmations aloud for two to three minutes. Make sure you're not just saying the words; you need to be present in the moment and believe what you are saying. You can save yourself some time by doing this in the shower too.
- Set aside five minutes within your day to stand in front of a mirror and repeat your affirmations. This can be incredibly powerful – look yourself in the eye and speak from the heart.
- Repeat your affirmations throughout the day as much as possible – people have busy lives but there's no reason why all the above cannot be used – you don't have to pick just one way.

One of the most useful ways to check whether your affirmations are helping is to incorporate some daily written reflections too. Each night, write down one thing that happened during the day that can be used as evidence to support you to believe your affirmations. For example, did someone give you a compliment?

Did you get some positive feedback? Don't just think this part – write it down! This is useful because when things get tough and you have a bad day or you're struggling with completing your affirmations, you can look back on the evidence that you have collected to help reaffirm that you are enough!

Incorporating positive affirmations can seem strange and daunting at first and sometimes you can feel a bit silly by having a go. But remember: these are for *you*. No one needs to know you're doing them, you don't have to shout them from your bedroom window every morning, and if you don't try – you'll never know whether it will help!

As with all goals and personal development tasks that you set yourself, it's important to reflect on your experiences to learn, make tweaks along the way if something isn't working for you and therefore continue moving forward.

Try the positive affirmations for two weeks, incorporating them into your daily life wherever you think they will fit and in whatever way works for you. After the two-week period, reflect on your experiences. Think about the following:

+ How did you feel completing your affirmations?
+ Do you feel differently now the two weeks are over?
+ What worked well for you in relation to incorporating the affirmations into your routine?
+ Was there anything you would change? If so, make that change and try again.
+ Is this something that you think will help you reach your goals?
+ What was the best moment you had in these last two weeks? Did you collect any evidence to back up your positive affirmations?
+ Does this work for you? Do you want to continue with it? If so, you can incorporate this into your daily/weekly/monthly goals further in the chapter.

Write down your two-week review here:

....
....
....
....
....
....
....

....

....

....

....

....

If this is something that you want to continue to use, write down the SMART goal that will help you continue to incorporate this into your life:

....

....

Personal reflections

Another strategy that you can use to help improve your self-esteem is personal reflections. The concept of this is that you reflect on every single day and write down between one and three positive things that have happened or that you feel are important and related to your self-esteem. Examples might be your boss giving you some good feedback on a piece of work you have done, a friend saying something positive about you, a partner giving you a compliment, or noticing a change in the way you think about yourself – for instance, you might have noticed that you are starting to be more positive in general. Whatever it is, every night, get into the habit of reflecting on your day.

Have a journal and keep it by your bed. You don't need to write enormous amounts of information, and it doesn't matter how big or small it is. Keeping your journal by your bed will remind you to complete your reflections every night. Even if you've had a bad day, it's always nice to end it by reflecting on the positives that have happened. If you have had a tough day, you got yourself through it, and that will have taken strength, perseverance and determination – telling yourself this is likely to improve self-esteem.

Try it now to give yourself an idea of how you might feel. What three things can you pick out of either today or the last few days that you have achieved? These can be *anything*, big or small:

1. ....

2. ....

3. ....

Rebecca Bernstein of the University of Touro explains that every thought has a chemical impact on the brain. When you think positively, this encourages the release of chemicals such as serotonin.[4] Serotonin is associated with feeling happy and calm, more focused and more emotionally stable. When you think negative thoughts, this increases the cortisol that is produced. Cortisol is the stress hormone and contributes to you feeling anxious and stressed. Chronic stress is particularly bad for your health in many ways. So positive thinking isn't just a way of looking at the world from a different perspective: it has a profound impact on the brain as well as your health and therefore will affect how you react to life too.

Positive thinking doesn't mean that you have to look at the world through rose-tinted glasses. Day-to-day life as a gender diverse person throws up so many barriers and so thinking positively every day can be challenging. Practising using a solution-focused mindset can support you to relieve stress, increase Serotonin and find a way forward, especially through those days that might feel endless.

TOP TIP

A 'bad day' is another opportunity to learn more about yourself and your strengths. Getting through a bad day is a reflection of your strength and determination.

Visualisations

Visualisation is using your imagination to picture yourself achieving your goal or being in a different state to your current one. It is a powerful tool that can be used in different ways to achieve different goals, not just for improving self-esteem; you'll see that it's used throughout this book in different chapters.

Visualisation is the process of picturing or imagining your preferred future or state in the case of self-esteem and confidence. As an example, if you're looking to improve your confidence, you might use visualisation as a way of imagining yourself as a confident person; maybe you are standing up taller or challenging someone's beliefs about you or standing up for yourself because you deserve to be respected by others.

Visualisation can be used for both short- and long-term goals. It can even be used to help boost your confidence immediately before you do a piece of work, enter a meeting or give a presentation. Visualisation helps you to believe in yourself, which is essential for reaching your goals.

You can build visualisation into your daily life in different ways. For example, you can use visualisation as part of your morning routine to imagine your bigger

---

4   https://tuw.edu/health/how-stress-affects-the-brain

goals and your preferred future, or you can visualise the day ahead and how you want the day to go. This can help to shape your day, because you already know the outcome you want – therefore you're more likely to work towards that during the day.

You can also take a couple of minutes for visualisation before a meeting or presentation or something you're nervous about that you want to go well. For a presentation, for instance, you can visualise the end with people clapping you, you having delivered your best possible work. This helps to increase your confidence just before you dive into that moment and can help reduce nervousness, encouraging you to perform better.

If you feel visualisation will work for you, it can be done anywhere, anytime, which is why it is so useful – think about some of the ways in which you could build visualisation into your daily life and note them here:

1. ....

2. ....

3. ....

If you're using visualisation to help to achieve your bigger yearly goals, you might not see much progress after two weeks. Instead make sure you use visualisation to realise or achieve something you need to do over the next two weeks so you can check whether you feel this will work for you. As in previous chapters, breaking down your goals into smaller chunks helps you track your progress, learn along the way and meet your overall objective.

When you're ready to review your progress, reflect on how you think this strategy has worked for you. Consider the following: is visualisation a useful strategy? What worked well? What would need to change for this to work better? Do you prefer building this into your daily life or do you like to use visualisation at key points?

....

....

....

....

....

....

....

....

....

....

....

....

One of the best strategies to use for goal setting is to identify the preferred future (as you've already done) and then work backwards from that goal. Visualisation is a tool we can use to help you achieve your preferred future.

So, thinking back to your preferred future, what do you want to have achieved in one year's time that would reflect you either achieving your preferred future or moving towards it? What would you be doing, thinking or feeling at this point in your life?

....

....

....

....

....

....

Working backwards from this timeframe now, and if you were on track with your progress towards reaching your preferred future, what evidence of progress would you have in six months' time? What would a six-month milestone towards your one-year goal look like? How would your thoughts or feelings reflect your progress?

....

....

....

....

....

....

Now it's time to break this down even further. What would you be seeing, thinking or feeling about yourself in three months' time, working backwards again from your preferred future? What would the milestone look like at three months when working towards your six- to twelve-month goal?

....

....

....

....

....

....

Using the same principles, what would you be seeing, thinking or feeling about yourself in one month's time if you were on track to meeting your self-esteem and confidence goals in one year's time? What would the one-month milestone look like?

....

....

....

....

....

....

You're already starting to see the underlying structures towards setting yourself a goal. These planning stages using visualisation are crucial to ensuring that you're setting yourself a goal that is SMART and therefore achievable.

Now consider the actions you'll need to take to reach your one-month, three-month, six-month and twelve-month goals/preferred future. To do this we'll use a similar small steps approach, breaking down the goals into achievable actions.

Consider your one-month goal now and split this into four weeks. If your actions are SMART for this next part, you'll know whether your one-year goal was SMART in the first place; if you've set yourself an unrealistic target for one year, this will be evidenced in your smaller weekly goals. If you are unsure, have a read over the SMART goal-setting notes in the values section in Chapter 6.

What do you need to do each week for four weeks to achieve your one-month goal?

....

....

....

....

Before you move on to the next section, reflect on what you have written. Is it *Specific* enough? Is it *Measurable*? Is it *Achievable*? Is it *Realistic*? Is it *Timely*? Does it feed into your one-year goal? For example, if you do those actions for 52 weeks, building on them as you go along, will you achieve your goal for the year?

Be honest with yourself. Remember – it's only you that can achieve your goals, so give yourself the opportunity to do so by getting this part right.

Next think about your three-month goal, using the same principles. What do you need to do each day? What do you need to do each week to reach your three-month goal? Write this down here:

....

....

....

....

....

....

Next, consider your six-month goal: what do you need to do each day/week/month to achieve your six-month goal that builds on the progress you have already made?

....

....

....

....

....

....

And once you've reached your six-month goal, what would you then need to do to move forward towards your one-year goal? Write it down here:

....

....

....

....

....

....

Tracking progress

At each of these points, you will need to know whether you are on track to reach your goals, and to do this you should use regular reviews. Tracking progress is essential to reaching your goals. If you don't track your progress, you won't be able to tell whether you have achieved your goal, so how will you know if you're working towards your preferred future? You don't want to end up in a situation where you find yourself having achieved a goal that you didn't set for yourself because you didn't track your progress.

Tracking progress also helps you to reflect on what you have achieved, keeps you motivated, reminds you of what you are working towards in relation to your preferred future, and helps you learn more about yourself and what works for you. It is important when you are tracking progress that you conduct regular reviews. That way, if you need to make any changes to keep you on track or you have unexpectedly achieved over and above what you wanted to in a certain timeframe, you can review your goals, amend the plan and continue on the trajectory that works for you.

Reviewing progress

Monthly reviews of your goals are one way to track progress because you have set your goals based on timeframes, for example one month, three months, six months, one year. Use the review tool below at appropriate intervals to see what you have achieved.

Month.....................................

What have you achieved this month? What are you proud of? What were your best moments?

1. ....

2. ....

3. ....

4. ....

5. ....

On reflection, was there anything that could have been done better? Or is there anything you could change that you think will help you in the future?

1. ....

2. ....

3. ....

4. ....

5. ....

On a scale of 1–10, 1 being 'I didn't move towards my goals', 10 being 'I achieved everything I set out to', how well have you achieved last month's goals?

(1)　(2)　(3)　(4)　(5)　(6)　(7)　(8)　(9)　(10)

What do you think you can do to move one point up the scale next month?

....

....

....

....

You can either do this task monthly or weekly depending on what works best for you. If you choose to review your progress weekly or on short timescales, ensure you also conduct a wider review at key intervals such as halfway through and towards the end of the timeframe you set yourself for achieving the goal.

Once you have reviewed your progress, you'll need to also review your goals again. It might be that you need to set yourself smaller goals, or you might have achieved your goals already, in which case you'll need to set yourself some new goals. Either way, review your goals and complete a plan for the following month. Remember – you are working towards your preferred future and one-year goal, so ensure your smaller goals reflect this. Use the SMART acronym to write new goals if you need to.

Planning your next steps

What goals are you aiming to achieve this month that will enable you to achieve your yearly goal?

1. ....

2. ....

3. ....

4. ....

5. ....

How confident do you feel you will achieve your goals this month?

(1) (2) (3) (4) (5) (6) (7) (8) (9) (10)

Based on last month's reflections, what commitments will you make to yourself to ensure that you reach your goals this month? Reflect on whether you need to be more organised, more committed, make more time to reach your goals or put a bit more effort in. Make a commitment to yourself here!

1. ....

2. ....

3. ....

4. ....

5. ....

How will you know that you will have achieved your monthly goal? What will be the indicators of success? How will you feel? Will there be a tangible outcome? What will have changed?

....

....

....

....

....

....

The second time that you come to review your goals, use your answer above to identify whether you have achieved what you set out to – do you feel like you did what you said you would? Have you got the tangible outcome? Did changes occur that you anticipated would happen? Is there other evidence you can use to state you've achieved your goals? Be accountable to yourself!

TOP TIP

Write a note in your diary or set a reminder on your phone to review your progress every month.

When you review your progress and plan your next steps, you'll need to be able to identify how you will know that you are on track.

When you plan your next month's goals, how will you know that you are on track to reach your one-year goal? Think back to the goal we worked through of writing a book. What should you be seeing two months in, bearing in mind the weekly goal was to write 1155 words? At two months in you should have written approximately 9240 words. You'll know whether you are on track by using indicators like this.

So, now that you've reviewed your progress and have planned your next month's goals, how will you know that you are on track? What will you have achieved in the next month that will indicate to you that you're going to reach your overall yearly goal?

1. ....

2. ....

3. ....

4. ....

5. ....

When you come to reviewing your progress after the next month, check the indicators you have written here to see if you're on track or if you've exceeded what you said you were going to achieve. This will help you to understand the next steps you need to take on your journey. Use this process each month as part of your reviews and planning.

When you review your progress, you should also identify how you feel looking back on your achievements. Did you think you would be able to achieve what you have set out to? Has anything surprised you? You've come so far and achieved so much already, how do you feel? What have you learnt about yourself that will help you reach your milestones for the next month?

....

....

....

....

....

....

> **TOP TIP**
> Tracking progress helps you to stay on track, reach your goals, and identify
> potential obstacles and strategies for how to overcome them. The more you
> track, the more you'll achieve!

Confidence

While self-esteem refers to the belief in ourselves as humans, our worthiness
and the value we place on ourselves, confidence is the belief that we have in our
abilities in different areas of our lives.

Self-confidence is essential throughout your journey towards achieving your
goals in life. Confidence in yourself and your abilities will help shape who you
are and support you to achieve your future goals. Confidence helps us to feel less
fear and anxiety, because it is the ability to believe that we can do what we set out
to, and it is the belief that even if we don't quite make it to the destination, we've
learnt many things along the way, and it doesn't deter us from moving forward.

Lack of confidence in yourself can lead to perpetuating negative thoughts
and feelings, believing that you have nothing to offer the world. You may also
experience lower levels of resilience, lack of self-care and struggles with personal
relationships as well as believing you are powerless to make any changes in your
life. Lack of confidence can also lead to perpetuating your limiting beliefs.

Confidence also helps us to experience higher levels of motivation, more resilience to overcome barriers and to feel a sense of congruence in relation to living
authentically.

It is important to find balance in relation to self-confidence: too little and
you're less likely to achieve your goals, too much and you may become inflexible,
not taking other opinions into account, therefore missing opportunities to learn
and develop.

Confidence can be learnt and developed over time, and when practised alongside the strategies you've learnt in the self-esteem section, will leave you feeling
like you can conquer the world and realise your dreams. It's important to try out
lots of different strategies when looking to improve self-esteem and confidence
so you can identify what will help you on your journey and throw out the rest.

Power posing

When you're in need of a confidence boost to help you overcome something in your
life that's important to you, power posing will help you get there! Power posing is
the concept that standing in certain positions increases the feeling of confidence.
The concept is based on the idea that your body influences how you feel. If you're

slumped over, head down in a small position, your feelings and mood will reflect this. If you're standing tall, hands on your hips and head up high, your mood can be influenced by this. Power posing for two minutes every day can help to boost self-confidence and make you feel like you can take on whatever challenge you might be facing that day.

Power posing can be done anywhere, anytime. If you're heading into an important meeting and you need to feel a bit more confident, power posing before you go in can help give you a much-needed boost! You can incorporate this into your daily morning routines or use it throughout the day as and when required.

Self-respect

Self-respect is just as important as self-confidence. Self-respect reflects our values and ethics as a human: what we're willing to do and not willing to do in relation to our overall life plans. Self-respect guides us from within and affects our behaviour and actions. People with higher levels of self-respect are more likely to make decisions that are based on their personal values and ethics and likely to be positive and work for them. People with lower levels of self-respect may exhibit more destructive behaviours which don't support them on their path towards realising their dreams.

Self-respect is intricately linked to self-esteem in that it is an understanding of whether we value ourselves and our contribution to the world. Self-respect is an important tool to have on your personal development journey; it will help you make decisions that are right for you when you're faced with barriers you need to overcome. Incorporating a good self-care routine helps to build self-respect.

Self-fulfilling prophecy

The self-fulfilling prophecy refers to holding a belief about yourself or your circumstances and constantly looking to gain evidence to confirm that belief. This can be a very damaging thought process to have, particularly if you are constantly berating yourself and listening to your limiting beliefs. When you find evidence that backs up your limiting beliefs, this feeds into your inability to move forward towards your goals. You believe you can't achieve what you'd like to because of a set of circumstances or barriers in your way – you believe that you can't overcome these barriers because you now have evidence to back up your limiting beliefs. Equally, if you believe in yourself and your abilities to achieve your potential, you'll look for evidence to confirm this and will find the evidence because you'll be taking action and achieving your smaller goals that feed into your bigger goals – so it can be a very powerful process if used correctly.

If you believe you can reach a small goal you've set yourself and you take action to move towards this goal, you'll achieve it – therefore you've created the evidence necessary to back up your claims that you can do this!

Self-fulfilling prophecy is something you should be constantly aware of, especially if you fall into the trap of believing your own limiting beliefs because this will hold you back. What's important to note here is that you *do* have a choice – you can either be your own worst enemy or your own best friend. Which will help you on your journey to success and which will hold you back? Make a conscious decision and be accountable for the decision that you have made. We can only ever be responsible for the choices that we make and not the behaviours of others.

SNAPSHOT

- Use the SMART process to make small, manageable goals that feed into your longer-term goals.
- Understanding your limiting beliefs will help you identify when you are playing into them and therefore help you move away from them.
- Work backwards from your bigger goals to identify the smaller steps – then act! When you do nothing, nothing happens!
- You can't expect others to believe in you if you don't believe in yourself.
- Set your goals, track your progress and review your achievements at key intervals. When you track progress, you're more likely to achieve your goals. Your mid-point indicators will tell you whether you're on track to realising your potential.
- Whether you believe you can or you believe you can't – you're right.

Chapter 4

Health

Being in a state of overall good health is the single most important thing that can support you to reach your goals. Everybody is different and prioritising your overall health is important, and can support you to reach your full potential. No matter what health goals you might want to achieve, the mind and body are complex systems and supporting yourself to manage stress can improve your life in many ways. Managing stress, eating well and exercising regularly are the essential components of overall good health. Busy and stressed people can sometimes skip meals, not exercise, and focus all their time and energy on their work or other things in their life. They may find it hard to muster up the energy to do anything else that sits outside of their core priorities, and this can lead people to burnout. Burnout and stress are two of the most significant health challenges that people will face in the modern-day world, and learning to manage these is crucial to reaching your full potential. Exercise and eating well gives people more energy; it's this 'extra' energy that you can then use to your advantage to start working on your goals.

Setting yourself health goals or challenges can help you move towards achieving something you might not have thought possible beforehand and will help you to start improving your self-esteem and confidence. Achieving a health or fitness goal can be rewarding and may give you a sense of accomplishment if health and fitness is something you wish to prioritise – leading you to believe in yourself more and challenge yourself in ways you might not have done previously.

If your body and mind are working together in harmony, you'll be able to think more clearly and be more productive generally, either at home, work or school – giving yourself an advantage over your peers.

When you apply the strategies in this chapter to your life, you'll reach fitness and wellness goals that you never thought were possible before. You'll feel and see the benefits of prioritising your health and wellbeing, and you'll feel better!

Prioritising health for gender diverse people is also crucial if you're likely to undertake any medical treatment in relation to transition. Not all gender diverse people wish to have surgery (and that's okay!) but for those that do, there are health goals that surgical teams highlight to their patients as important for some surgical procedures. These are requirements that are set by NHS teams. As with any surgical procedures, the fitter you are going into surgery, the more likely it will be that your recovery will be smoother. With all surgery there is a risk of complications, but the healthier you are when you do have surgery, the more likely you'll be to have a positive result limiting the risk of complications.

Surgical procedures in relation to transition are incredibly complex and intricate, and this is why, for example, some surgical teams stipulate that patients quit smoking and have a good level of general health before they receive confirmation that surgery can go ahead. Waiting times for surgery are equally just as difficult to manage from a mental health perspective, therefore prioritising your health and fitness can support you to mentally prepare for surgery as well as being able to manage the impact that being on long waiting lists for surgery can have on wellbeing. Not all gender diverse people will undertake surgery for many different reasons; however, if you do wish to pursue health and wellness goals for other reasons, then this section can support you to do that.

The first and most important thing you need to know about yourself before you start writing your goals is whether you have the determination to change something. Do you have what it takes to go the extra mile, to get up a bit earlier to reach your goals, to push yourself and see what you're capable of? Take some time to reflect on this. What do you know about yourself that will help you achieve your health and wellbeing goals? Think back to the discussion about personal values and standards in Chapter 1: what will help you here? Use statements such as 'I have/am/can…':

....

....

....

....

....

....

Check in with yourself. Where is your health and fitness right now? Do you want to lose weight, put on weight, reduce alcohol intake or quit smoking? These are just examples, choose what's right for you.

....

....

....

....

....

....

Let's look back at the preferred futures exercise completed in the previous chapter. When you visualise your future self in relation to your health and fitness, what does this look like? What have you achieved? Are you standing on a podium holding up a medal? Have you just finished a marathon? Do you imagine getting that great time logged on your fitness app? Or are you hoping to get confirmation that surgery can go ahead? You might want to quit smoking and be happy with that as your goal – it doesn't matter how big or small your preferred future is; it just needs to be personal to you and no one else. Write down your preferred future here:

....

....

....

....

....

....

You'll have seen many stories of people achieving amazing things in their lives: overcoming the odds and coming through to achieve something that onlookers thought was impossible – it all comes down to whether you believe you can achieve your goals, you're willing to put in the work and you can keep your eyes on the prize.

Many people have gone through a process of change before and have struggled to reach their goals. If this sounds like you, knowing what the barriers were and being aware of them will help you prepare to overcome them in the future, instead of falling at the first hurdle.

Learning from your own experience is important so that you can understand yourself on a deeper level and be able to move forward and overcome barriers in the future. If you know what might stop you in your tracks this time, you can plan for this, be more prepared and overcome it this time round. You'll reach new heights, and you'll be able to re-evaluate what you thought you were capable of.

Think back to a time when you've tried to make positive changes to your health before. What happened?

....

....

....

....

....

....

Why did you stop on your journey towards change? What barriers were put in your way?

....

....

....

....

....

....

What do you know about yourself that will help you overcome these barriers in the future? Think about the work you've already done on your strengths, for example, in previous chapters:

....

....

....

....

....

....

Using a strengths-based approach to affirmations can help you when you're struggling to complete a workout or even struggling to get out of the door to start working on your health goals – saying your affirmations to yourself can give you the strength, motivation and determination to move forward and make some progress.

Stress

Stress is one of the many reasons why people struggle on their journey towards change. Stress can come in many different forms; it can be the catalyst for negative behaviour and struggles towards change. Sometimes stress can motivate us, other times it can be incredibly destructive. According to the NHS,[1] you might see and feel the following:

Physical symptoms	Mental symptoms	Changes in behaviour
Headache/dizziness	Difficulty concentrating	Being irritable and snappy
Muscle tension or pain	Struggling to make decisions	Sleeping too much or too little
Stomach problems	Feeling overwhelmed	Eating too much or too little
Chest pain/faster heartbeat	Constantly worrying	Avoiding certain places/people
Sexual problems	Being forgetful	Drinking/smoking more

As seen above, stress can re-trigger things like smoking for example, because you've had a bad day. How does stress affect you? What do you notice about yourself when you are feeling stressed? Does this trigger negative behaviours, thoughts or feelings for you? Write down your observations here. If you're struggling to think of what happens, ask someone you trust to tell you what they see when you are stressed:

....
....
....
....
....
....

To ensure you don't reach a point where your behaviour becomes destructive, can you identify any early warnings signs? If you start to binge eat, not eat or binge drink alcohol, for example, how can you identify this early so you then don't start to see and feel other symptoms or stress? Often when people start to experience the symptoms of stress this can spiral out of control very quickly, so identifying the early warning signs can help prevent destruction because you'll be more aware of when things might be slipping out of control. Write down your early warning signs here:

....

---

1 www.nhs.uk/mental-health/feelings-symptoms-behaviours/feelings-and-symptoms/stress

....

....

....

....

....

The more self-awareness we have about our behaviours, thoughts and feelings, the easier it will be to identify when things might be slipping for you and therefore how you can get yourself back on track towards achieving your goals.

Self-care

Self-care is a term that we're hearing more and more about recently and might involve eye-rolling whenever someone says it to you! But it isn't to be underestimated. Self-care is crucial to personal development; it is the foundation from which you can build your preferred future. For you to reach your potential, you've got to get the basics right first. If you're not looking after yourself, it will affect how you feel about yourself. To reach your goals, you must have a solid foundation to work from. Think of it like a house – you must have a solid foundation to work from otherwise your house will fall and crumble if it isn't well looked after.

Start by developing a morning routine and sticking to it! If you're trying to go for that big promotion or trying to get your life back on track, self-care is the place to start!

Let's look at your basic needs first. These fall into three categories: diet, exercise and sleep.

Diet

What does your diet currently look like? Think about the following and be honest:

How many calories do you eat each day?...

What is the content of the calories?..

Are you eating enough fruit and vegetables? (Five portions per day are recommended.)..

What time do you eat?...

Do you skip meals and binge eat instead? ....

How do you currently feel about your diet? Does it require improvement? What do you want to change?

....
....
....
....
....
....

How will the changes that you want to make have a positive impact on your life?

....
....
....
....
....
....

Poor nutrition can contribute to low mood, stress and irritability as well as long-term health conditions such as obesity, diabetes and heart disease. A healthy diet helps to maintain the body physically and mentally, enabling you to operate on a more productive level. So, it's easy to see why diet is an essential foundation for personal development. If you're struggling with the effects of having a poor diet, you'll find it difficult to have the energy and therefore motivation to achieve more in your life.

There are plenty of diets out there that promise fast weight-loss results in a matter of weeks – these are not long-term, sustainable solutions. For those of you that might have struggled with weight gain/yo-yo dieting, you may have done so because you were looking for the short-term and quick-fix solutions. Like many aspects of this book, the short-term solution isn't going to bring you the lasting change you want. Small steps = big results.

If you're sticking to a set number of calories each day, that means you're sticking to that amount per week, per month and per year. If the number of calories that you are consuming is more than the energy you are burning, you'll gain weight. It's important to understand basic principles of weight management and build on them to personalise your weight management goals. Considering any individual requirements with support from your local healthcare team will tailor your plan to you and support you on your journey.

Planning, commitment, goals and small steps will help you reach your targets. There are maximum weight limits that surgeons recommend for people who are planning to undergo gender reassignment surgery, so if you are medically transitioning, it's important to be within those weight brackets so that you're not disappointed in the future. Whilst there are significant issues with waiting times for surgical procedures being too long, try to use this as an opportunity to work on your health goals, because whether you are looking to improve your mental health or physical health, progress takes time. Having a health goal whilst you wait for surgery can give you a focus and something to aim for, taking your mind off the waiting times and keeping you emotionally and mentally healthy in the process. So, with this in mind, let's look at how you can achieve your health goals.

Always consult the surgical team or gender identity clinic in relation to diet and weight if this is an issue for you, before you start any diet programme. Many people who are waiting for surgery have been told to lose weight and it is a challenging aspect of transitioning. If this is something you are struggling with, then here are a few strategies that might help support you on your journey.

According to the NHS Live Well Weight Loss guide, a healthy amount of weight to aim to lose is approximately 1lb per week.

What is your current weight? ....

What is your ideal weight? ....

At the time of writing, Gender Reassignment surgical teams are still using the BMI model to assess weight and eligibility for surgery. Whilst it has been widely discredited, teams are still using it and this can be a barrier to accessing surgery. If you're unsure what your ideal weight should be, visit the NHS BMI healthy weight calculator online.[2] Speak to your surgical team if your goals are based around eligibility for surgery or engage your local nursing practice for advice and guidance.

What is your timeframe for your target weight loss? ....

Many people who struggle with weight loss have tried a lot of diets, multiple times, and it can be incredibly frustrating and disappointing when you don't reach the goal that you set yourself. It's important to recognise what stopped you from continuing your weight-loss journey so that you can put in place some strategies to help you overcome potential barriers.

---

2 www.nhs.uk/live-well/healthy-weight/bmi-calculator

What has stopped you from reaching your weight-loss goals before? Think about the last time you tried to lose weight; what were the triggers that stopped you in your tracks? They might be things like stress, emotional eating, powerful feelings and work. Note them here:

. . . .

. . . .

. . . .

. . . .

. . . .

. . . .

This is the time to be honest with yourself. If you can't be, you'll struggle in the next stages when you come to planning for your weight-loss journey. If you can't identify what your real triggers are and be honest as to why you struggle to stay on track, you're likely to hit the same barriers and find it hard to overcome them again.

Having identified what your triggers are, use the visualisation techniques discussed earlier to imagine what you could put in place next time you hit a similar barrier.

For example, if stress is a trigger for you, you have a busy lifestyle and no time to cook, so you find yourself calling for a takeaway on the way home, why not try to batch cook some meals and freeze them? That way, when you're in a hurry you can heat up a meal instead and still eat well on the days you are struggling.

If you eat for comfort, can you identify what might help you feel better instead? You could try drinking a whole glass of water before choosing to eat anything or even going out for a brisk walk, reading a book or watching something on TV. Alternatively, if TV is a trigger for you, set yourself a time-limit goal, for example no eating after 6.30 in the evening, to stop the snacking.

It's also useful to note that eating too little will have a negative impact on your health. You might lose weight but it's important to be healthy, and weight in and of itself is not necessarily a direct indicator of overall good health.

Here are some tips that might help you:

Problem	Solution
Watching TV, eating without thinking	Set yourself a time limit that you don't eat after
	Have a drink of water instead of eating snacks
	Choose healthy snacks, e.g. fruit
	Ask yourself if you are hungry, or bored

cont.

Problem	Solution
Eating too much	Download a calorie tracker – input *every* calorie you eat
	Start a food diary to identify exactly how many calories you are eating
Thinking you don't eat too much	Start a food diary and input everything you eat generally in front. one week – don't change anything at first, add up the calories and see if these are within the healthy ranges
Too little time	Batch cook
	Plan your meals
	Shop for the week, not just for a few days at a time
Too much time	Shop for the week
	Plan your meals
	Plan your meals by calories – split them and snacks across your calorie allowance
	Be productive with your time in between meals
	Drink a glass of water when you think you want to eat outside of mealtimes
Self-esteem/confidence	Work through the self-esteem and confidence chapter of the book
	Set yourself some goals within that chapter, alongside a weight-loss goal – small steps
Not eating enough	Start a food diary, identify everything that you eat
	Consider foods that have a higher calorie and nutrient density to reach your calorie allowance

What are your triggers?

....

....

....

....

....

....

What strategies will you use to help you overcome these triggers when they occur?

....

....

....

....

....

....

Like most things in life, preparation is key, and it is an essential skill in general if you're going to manage multiple goals and reach your potential. Understanding yourself and reflecting on previous experiences and barriers can support you with your future goals. We learn from our experiences and failures in the same way we learn from our successes. Understanding what works for you and doesn't work for you and incorporating that into your plan gives you a stronger foundation to reach your goals. If stress is a trigger, plan for this and stick to what you said you were going to do. You can only be responsible for yourself, and your actions will determine the outcome.

It's also important to note that the types of food you're eating will determine your level of performance. If you're constantly eating junk food, expect lower levels of energy and lack of performance generally in many aspects of your life. You'll struggle to reach your goals if you don't have the energy to focus, prepare and deliver on what you said you would do.

If cooking skills are holding you back from preparing simple, healthy meals, why not consider setting yourself a goal to help you learn? There are many resources on YouTube that teach people step by step how to cook healthy meals. You could sign up to a local cookery course or even to a Skill Share programme whereby someone can show you how to cook in exchange for you teaching them a skill you might have. Remember to make sure your goal is SMART. Cooking healthy meals can often save you money in comparison to purchasing convenience foods that are typically the less healthy option and will affect your energy levels and performance generally.

Let's look at how you will achieve your goal. Again, we're using the SMART acronym to help you – ensuring success if you follow the steps.

Working backwards from your main goal, what weight do you want to achieve by six months, three months, one month?

6 months ....

3 months ....

1 month...................................

Following on from your one-month goal, what do you need to do each week to get you to that goal? Based on the NHS guidelines, you should be aiming to lose 1lb per week, 4lbs per month.

....

....

....

....

....

....

How many calories per day do you need to reach your one-month goal? ....

If you're not sure what calorie range you need to be in, check out the NHS website.[3] If you're pre-/post-hormone treatment, speak to your local healthcare provider to ask their advice in relation to what calorie allowance would work best for you. Hormones are incredibly powerful and affect people in different ways. For example, trans men who have been taking testosterone for a couple of years may benefit from following the guidelines for men, but someone pre-testosterone might be eating too much if they follow these guidelines. Everybody is different so will need different advice and guidance depending on what their health goals are and any health conditions that also need to be managed simultaneously.

It's important to have a plan if you're embarking on a weight-loss journey. Check out these tips to help you formulate a strategy that will work for you:

- Plan out every meal and snack for the week and shop for that in one go. Don't go shopping when you're hungry – you're more likely to buy things outside of your plan!
- Consider batch cooking if you don't have much time on your hands, and freeze leftovers for quick meals.
- Download a calorie-counting app and track all your calories every day. It's hard at first to input everything but the app will remember what you input so it gets easier to track your calories.
- Fill your diet with healthy foods that work for you and that help you to manage any dietary restrictions you may have. Also remember to pick foods you like to eat! This might be an opportunity for you to try new foods too! Get some advice from your local GP nursing team or the NHS website for further information.

---

3 www.nhs.uk/common-health-questions/food-and-diet

[X] Stay off the scales. You don't need to weigh yourself every day; this can be demotivating. Weight can fluctuate throughout the day depending on a whole range of factors. Stick to the same weigh-in time and day each week and record your progress on your calorie tracker app.

[X] Write down your meal plan where you can see it so it's easy to refer to if you struggle to remember it.

[X] Use a snack box. Plan your snacks the day before and put them in a lunch box; only eat what you've put in there to keep you within your calorie range.

[X] Make your meals the day before, especially if you've got a busy schedule the following day.

Following on from these tips, what strategies will you implement to help you with your weight goals? You don't have to pick just one:

....

....

....

....

....

What do you need to do each week to achieve your goal?

....

....

....

....

....

Based on your weekly goal, what do you then need to do each day to achieve your goal?

....

....

....

....

....

You can use this planner to help you. Make a copy each week and put it where you'll see it. Planning out what you'll eat and the calorie content of each meal and snack will help you stay on track.

	Breakfast	Snack	Lunch	Snack	Dinner	Snack	Water (1.2–1.5l per day)	Total calories
Monday								
Tuesday								
Wednesday								
Thursday								
Friday								
Saturday								
Sunday								

Water intake is extremely important. The NHS recommends you should drink at least six to eight glasses of water per day to replenish water lost throughout the day.[4] This is approximately 1.2 to 1.5 litres a day. Drinking water instead of tea, coffee, alcohol or fizzy drinks can help you maintain a healthy weight. These drinks have a high calorie content, so switching to water is a great way to reduce your calorie intake and give your body what it needs to function. If you struggle to drink water or don't like the taste, try sparkling water with a lemon or lime slice or low-calorie, low-sugar squash as an alternative. Drinking plenty of water can help flush out toxins in the body, promote weight loss and promote increased energy. Access Health states your brain is mainly water, so drinking plenty can help you remain focused and able to think and concentrate better.[5]

One-month review

Once you have reached the one-month point, complete the following section.

Did you achieve your goal?

....

If not, what are your reflections on why not? Were there any significant barriers? Was the goal achievable?

....

....

....

....

....

....

How do you feel about your progress so far?

....

....

....

....

---

4 www.nhs.uk/live-well/eat-well/water-drinks-nutrition
5 https://accesshealthla.org/top-5-benefits-drinking-water

Is there anything you would do differently in the next month?

....

....

....

....

....

....

Do you feel you are on track to reach your two-month goal?

....

What can you do to ensure you reach your two-month goal?

....

....

....

....

....

....

Remember: if you're struggling at this point, review your original goals. If you feel they were not manageable for whatever reason, then scale them back to smaller, more achievable goals. We all have other commitments in our lives whether that's looking after family members, caring for others, studying, working and much more. This is a personal journey and it's okay to scale back your goals into smaller steps to make them achievable and sustainable in the long term.

On a scale of 1 to 10, 1 being not at all confident, 10 being as confident as you could be, how confident do you feel that you will reach your two-month goals?

(1) (2) (3) (4) (5) (6) (7) (8) (9) (10)

Is there anything you feel that you can do or put in place to help you feel more confidence for next month? If so, what will you commit to?

....

....

....

....

When will you do this by?

....

Does this conform to the SMART principles?

....

Can you put anything else in place to ensure this is the next *smallest* step towards your goal? Identify that here:

....

....

....

....

On a scale of 1 to 10, 1 being not at all confident, 10 being as confident as you could be, how confident do you feel after implementing further strategies to support you in your second month?

(1) (2) (3) (4) (5) (6) (7) (8) (9) (10)

Thinking about your next month's goals, what is the first step you will take?

....

....

Identify the steps you will take in order to reach your two-month goals:

....

....

....

....

....

....

Remember to use time to split up your tasks into manageable chunks, for example week to week or day to day; make sure you work backwards from your goal to identify the steps you'll take.

How will you know that you have been successful in reaching your two-month goals? What indicators will you have of your success?

....

....

....

....

Using visualisation techniques to identify potential barriers can help you mitigate these by planning for them. Visualise any barriers you may encounter and use this as an opportunity to plan for these occurrences and break through them to reach your goals.

Do you anticipate any barriers to reaching your next set of goals? If so, what are they?

....

....

....

....

What plans can you put in place to overcome these barriers should they arise?

....

....

....

....

Exercise

Exercise is crucial to our wellbeing, whether we are trying to lose weight or just generally improve our health. Exercise helps us to maintain a healthy body and mind and should be something you incorporate into your daily and weekly routines to keep you performing at your best. Exercise also helps to relieve and manage stress and can take many forms. It helps you to feel mentally and physically stronger, and if you set yourself personal goals it can give you a sense of achievement and drive towards reaching other goals in your life.

The NHS advises that regular exercise can boost your mood.[6] Exercise causes chemical changes in the brain which help to improve mood; this is especially useful if you're vulnerable to issues such as depression and anxiety. Exercise should be enjoyable otherwise it can be difficult to motivate yourself to build this into a routine.

Many people have been put off exercise because of trauma experienced in early childhood, at school for example, particularly those who are gender diverse. These experiences can include having to get changed in front of peers, not being able to participate in sport with peers of the same gender and not enjoying the sports or games that are taught as part of the school curriculum. This can lead to inactivity in adulthood, weight gain, mental health issues and lack of motivation to exercise generally.

It can be difficult to take on new challenges and exercise. For gender diverse people, exercise can be challenging due to issues such as binding and tucking. Exercising safely is extremely important in order to minimise issues associated with binding and tucking.

Here are some tips to get you started:

- Work out at home – if you feel you don't want to take up things like running, sports classes or using a gym, there are plenty of workouts you can use at home. You might feel more comfortable exercising if you're in your own space.
- Choose appropriate clothing for the exercise you are doing; sports underwear is particularly useful and can help you feel less dysphoric – ask for recommendations from others who exercise regularly.
- Walking is a great way to incorporate exercise into your daily life without compromising on binding and tucking – invest in a good pair of walking shoes to support your feet and enable you to walk further or faster. Even just being outside in nature can help promote positive mental health.

Exercise doesn't have to mean buying an expensive gym membership; there are plenty of free alternatives such as outdoor public gyms and YouTube workouts including exercises such as yoga, HIIT training, and skill and sport development. Strength training can be done at home with a set of weights and sometimes these are given away for free on recycling/sharing websites. You can also try calisthenic workouts – these are strength-based workouts that rely on your own body weight rather than equipment.

If you're someone that likes a challenge and finds it motivating to sign up to

6 www.nhs.uk/mental-health/self-help/guides-tools-and-activities/five-steps-to-mental
   -wellbeing

an event, then have a look around in your local area and see what's on offer. From park runs to marathons, Tough Mudder events to cycling events and triathlons – there's something for everyone. Signing up to raise money for a charity that's close to your heart can be a big motivator. Charities often offer places in events if you meet the minimum fundraising targets, so get in touch with a charity you want to support and find out what's on offer. It can be easier to meet your goals if others are relying on you to come through for them. Signing up for a charity event can also give you a greater sense of purpose and commitment and the satisfaction of supporting your community.

Exercise can be challenging when there are additional barriers. Speak to your GP or local nursing care providers for advice on how exercise can be accessible for you. Personalised advice may support you on your health journey and social prescribing by healthcare providers is becoming more and more prevalent.

What is your overall goal in relation to exercise? What do you want to achieve?

....

....

....

....

How long do you think it will take you to achieve this?

....

Working backwards from this timeframe, set yourself four targets, splitting up your goal into four timeframes (for example, one month, two months, six months, one year). You can use a different timeframe – choose what is right for you based on your goal:

1. ....
2. ....
3. ....
4. ....

What evidence will there be to suggest you have met each of your targets?

1. ....
2. ....
3. ....
4. ....

What do you need to do to reach each target?

1. ....
2. ....
3. ....
4. ....

Now let's break this down further into weeks.

What do you need to do each week to reach your first milestone?

....
....
....
....
....
....

What evidence will there be each week to show you are on track?

....
....
....
....
....

Based on your weekly goals, what do you need to do each day to make sure you meet your targets? Use this weekly exercise planner below together with the weekly meal planner in the diet section earlier on in the chapter to help you.

Day	Exercise
Monday	
Tuesday	
Wednesday	
Thursday	
Friday	
Saturday	
Sunday	

As you achieve each of your targets from following your daily and weekly plans, use this planner to amend your daily and weekly targets, enabling you to reach your next milestones.

Your exercise and eating plans will depend on what you're trying to achieve. If you're training for an event, you can often find training plans available online that are broken down into manageable sections and easy to incorporate into your daily life. If you've signed up for a charity event, many fundraising departments have advice and information for people training for their events and are usually willing to support you on your journey as much as they can – so don't be afraid to get in touch.

To help you feel more prepared for the task ahead, set yourself some research goals as part of your personal development plan. These could be to look at different sports clubs that are on offer in the local community, to consult on trans health social networking groups to see what other people are involved in or to get some ideas about trans-friendly sports clubs. Get in touch with local LGBTQIA+ support services to find out about their programmes. In some places around the country, trans support groups offer closed swimming sessions and trans-only sports clubs, so if you're not feeling very confident, find out some more information and then make your decision. If you don't like using the phone, most clubs/sports provision/

trans groups have social media pages, websites and email addresses so get in touch using these methods instead.

Set yourself a planning a research goal. What do you need to do to find out about what's on offer locally?

....

....

....

....

When will you do this by?

....

Is this a realistic timeframe? If not, go back and make your target more specific/ achievable.

....

....

....

....

Is this achievable?

....

What evidence will you have to show you have achieved your planning and research goals?

....

....

....

....

....

....

Get into the habit of using the SMART way of goal setting for all your goals, breaking them down as much as possible into smaller bite-sized chunks so that they are achievable and realistic, and you'll soon see the results that you planned for.

Achieving smaller milestones feeds into your bigger goal and eventually, with hard work and determination, you'll achieve things you never thought were possible.

Whatever your health goals, it's important that you incorporate daily exercise to remain healthy, alongside good nutrition. There are plenty of nutrition programmes and regimes out there that offer quick fixes and big results in a short space of time – avoid these; managing health is a lifestyle choice and one that can't be bought in a month or two. The NHS offers excellent advice and guidance on diet, nutrition and exercise. Speak to your GP practice to get an appointment with a nurse. Some people may struggle with barriers such as existing health conditions, so it's important in these circumstances to take advice from healthcare professionals on how to start your journey to better overall wellbeing if this is something you're choosing to prioritise.

If you struggle to achieve the goals and interim targets you have set yourself, review your progress and focus on the things that you have achieved. Review progress using the SMART acronym to make sure that what you've set yourself is achievable and realistic. As you learn more about yourself, your goals might change. Don't be afraid to change them; you are the expert in your own life.

Sleep

Sleep is an essential part of everyday life. Sleep ensures the brain and body can rest and recover, so you can wake up in the morning ready to take on the day. Without sleep, our bodies and minds would suffer, as would our overall health. According to the NHS, long-term sleep issues can contribute to difficulty carrying out day to-day tasks, increased stress, poor diet choices and lack of energy throughout the day (which might lead you to cancel that workout session), and can make it a struggle to maintain relationships and social activities.[7] The choices we make every day help to shape our future selves so if you're not getting enough sleep, and this impacts on your day-to-day life, you might not be making the right decisions that will help you build your preferred future.

Prioritising each element of what it means to be healthy (diet, exercise and sleep), will mean you have a strong foundation to enable you to carry out your small daily steps and reach your goals. Starting hormone replacement therapy can impact on your sleep and overall wellbeing, so it is crucial at that stage of transition that sleep becomes a priority. Many people starting hormone therapy struggle with too much or too little sleep as the body starts to adjust itself. Ensure that you're aware of the impact that hormone therapy is having on your sleep routines, so you can adjust over time, enabling you to perform at your best!

---

7   https://www.nhs.uk/every-mind-matters/mental-health-issues/sleep

How many hours a day do you currently sleep?

....

Is this too little or too much?

....

What do you notice about yourself when you have too little sleep? For example, how do you feel the next day? How does this affect your performance and day-to-day life?

....

....

....

....

....

What do you notice about yourself when you have too much sleep?

....

....

....

....

....

What has worked for you previously in promoting good quality sleep?

....

....

....

....

....

What hasn't worked well for you in the past when practising good sleep routines?

....

....

....

....

....

....

Working until late at night and jumping straight into bed after being on technology can leave you feeling like your mind is still buzzing with work and you'll struggle to sleep. Also, if you don't leave yourself enough time to get good quality sleep, you'll struggle to perform at your best the next day. If you've got to be up for work in the morning at 8am and you're using technology until 4am, that only leaves you a potential window of 4 hours' sleep (which isn't enough).

The NHS recommends that adults need at least 7 to 9 hours' sleep every night.[8] There are many strategies you can use to improve your sleep routine and ensure you're getting the right amount of sleep. Some tips you might find useful to promote a strong sleep routine are:

- Plan what time you need to go to bed to ensure you'll have enough time to get enough sleep.
- Ensure your sleeping environment is free from stressful things, for example work items, reports or paperwork.
- Ensure the room is dark enough.
- Ensure there are no distractions – don't charge your phone by your bed, as you might choose to pick it up and scroll through social media if you can't sleep, instead of picking up a book instead.
- Wind down before you get to bed – get off technology at least an hour before you go to sleep and don't watch anything on the TV that's stress-inducing.
- Read for at least an hour before you go to bed.
- Use an alarm clock instead of your phone to wake you up in the morning.
- Ensure that an hour before you go to bed, you're doing something that relaxes you – this might be a good opportunity to try something like meditation.

> **TOP TIP**
> Winding down before bedtime and ensuring you have a sleep routine will increase your chances of having a better night's sleep.

---

8 https://www.nhs.uk/conditions/insomnia

From the list above or previous experience, is there anything you're doing now that you want to continue to do?

....

....

....

....

....

....

Is there anything new you'd like to try to incorporate?

....

....

....

....

Why is this important to you?

....

....

....

....

What benefits do you think this will have on your life?

....

....

....

....

Understanding the choices you make throughout the day and the impact that this might have on your sleep will help you to make better decisions on a day-to-day basis, which will prompt better sleep the following day and also increase your performance overall.

The following can have a significant impact on the quality and quantity of sleep you'll get each night:

✦ Consuming too much caffeine throughout the day.
✦ Consuming excessive amounts of alcohol.
✦ Not exercising or going outside during the day.
✦ Long naps during the day.
✦ Going to sleep and waking up at different times every day.
✦ Eating late in the evening.
✦ Spending excess amounts of time on technology, especially if you're using your devices right up until the time you go to bed.

Is there anything on this list that you currently do and want to change?

....
....
....
....

Thinking about the other exercises in this chapter above and what new strategies you'd like to try, answer the following questions.

What would you like to put in place or try to improve your sleep?

....
....
....
....
....
....

What do you need to do first? Do you need any resources or to remove anything from your room? If so, what?

....
....
....
....

What is your next step?

....

....

....

....

When will you start this?

....

For many people, trial and error is the way that people understand themselves and what works best for them. So, it might take you some time to figure out what works best for you. For each strategy you'll try, answer the following questions.

Identify the strategy you want to try:

....

....

....

....

When will you start this?

....

How long will you try this strategy for?

....

Review

Did the strategy you tried help improve your sleep?

....

What benefits did this bring for you?

....

....

....

....

If this strategy didn't work for you, what was the reason why?

....

....

....

....

Will you continue to use this strategy or try something new?

....

....

....

....

Start again from the review section with each strategy that you want to try. It will take some time to get into a routine that works for you, so don't be put off if you don't find the right routine and strategy straight away. Trial and error are an excellent opportunity to learn more about yourself, build stronger habits and benefit from good quality sleep that will help you perform at your best.

Once you've figure out which strategies work well for you, you can use this as an opportunity to set yourself some personal rules. These will differ for everyone – what's important here is that they are personal to you. Avoid negative statements such as 'I won't go on technology before bed'; instead, use positive statements such as 'I will read a book half an hour before I go to sleep'. Remember! Use the SMART principles to help you write your personal rules.

Write your personal rules here:

....

....

....

....

....

....

Former US Navy Seal Admiral William McRaven says that if you want to change the world, start off by making your bed every day.[9] This promotes starting the day with a small task that is achievable. It will encourage you to take on the next small task of the day, then the next and the next, until you've completed lots of small tasks thro ughout the day. Also, if you have a bad day, you can feel safe in the knowledge that if everything else went wrong, you did achieve one thing, which was to make your bed. This also has the added benefit of promoting a good sleep routine. If you're getting into a made bed every night, it can help you to relax and promote good quality sleep.

Drugs and alcohol

Participating in the use of recreational drugs and alcohol is the quickest way to stop your goals in their tracks, before even considering the significant health implications.

Alcohol is a particular challenge in modern-day life because it is socially acceptable and many people's social lives revolve around going to the pub with a couple of mates or a boozy weekend away. Using alcohol can become problematic and it's a very challenging issue to tackle, especially as many social events are centred around alcohol with very little sober sociable spaces available. When alcohol use tips into more hangovers than not, you'll struggle to be motivated to achieve your goals. You won't be performing at your best, you'll have less energy and you'll be nursing hangover symptoms a lot of the time. This will have a significant impact on your physical health, mental health and emotional wellbeing. Many people worry that stopping drinking will mean they'll lose their friends, but if all you do with your friends is drink, your relationships are based on that and you don't get the benefit of having mutual (sober) friendships, which can be incredibly powerful in helping you achieve your goals.

If you're embarking on a new journey towards better health, try to limit your drug and alcohol consumption, or reduce it to start with. If you're a heavy user, speak to a health professional before cutting down completely or going cold turkey as this can have a serious impact on your health as well. Use a small steps approach: your first health and wellbeing goal could be to make an appointment within a one-week timeframe to speak to a healthcare professional – your first smallest step!

Many gender diverse people struggle with drug and alcohol use, and this is fed by LGBTQIA+ culture. Many safe spaces that are identified for people are centred around bars and nightlife, particularly in cities, but if you do some research you'll find LGBTQIA+ sports groups and clubs, activities and social events to help you meet new people. There is a growing number of sober spaces popping up across

---

9 https://www.armyupress.army.mil/Journals/NCO-Journal/Archives/2019/March/
   Make-Bed

the country, so investing some time into finding out what resources are out there at your disposal will help you to make the positive changes you want.

There are many support services you can engage in to help you reduce your use of drugs and alcohol; engaging in a recovery programme can help you learn more about yourself, your identity and your potential. Meeting other people on similar journeys to recovery can be motivating, and mutual support can help you to meet your goals. You might meet someone who wants to achieve a similar goal to you in relation to health, in which case you can team up and support each other along the way.

If you're planning on having surgical intervention to help treat gender dysphoria, abstinence or reduction in consumption of drugs and alcohol is essential. The Nottinghamshire Centre for Treatment of Gender Dysphoria advises that anyone wishing to be referred to the service with a drug or alcohol issue must ensure this is being effectively managed before considering a referral.[10] This is due to the higher risks associated with undertaking hormone therapy and surgical interventions that misusing substances can bring. Smokers are at much higher risk of developing issues with healing post-surgery. According to Dr Scott Mosser (Gender Confirmation Centre), smoking inhibits the growth of blood vessels and constricts blood vessels, thus reducing the surgical site's oxygen supply, and delayed healing could result in a difficult recovery period, additional surgical procedures to rectify issues, and potentially a delayed return to work, leading to financial loss.[11] Scarring can be significantly worse, and smoking increases the risk of issues from anaesthesia.

Start to consider a recovery plan. What do you want to achieve?

....

....

....

....

....

....

How will you achieve this? (Consider support mechanisms; recovery is easier with support.)

---

10 www.nottinghamshirehealthcare.nhs.uk/nottingham-centre-for-transgender-health

11 https://www.genderconfirmation.com/blog/quitting-smoking/#:~:text=Dr.,rule%20that%20 must%20be%20followedj

....
....
....
....
....
....

What is your timeframe for your recovery goals?

....
....

Break this down into smaller steps, using a timeframe that suits you:

....
....
....
....
....
....

Who do you need to reach out to for support? (Friends/family/professionals/ support groups/online groups/face-to-face groups/gender diverse recovery groups, etc.)

....
....
....
....

What is your first step?

....
....

What are your next steps?

....

....

....

....

....

....

When will you take your first step?

....

Life is filled with ups and downs. Some days you might be really motivated to change things for yourself, other days can be more difficult. What barriers might you face when taking your next steps?

....

....

....

....

....

....

Visualise what you will do to overcome these barriers. Who can you reach out to for support? What tools can you use to help you through this difficult period?

....

....

....

....

....

....

Daily goals might become overwhelming, especially if you are trying to make significant changes in your life. You can break down your daily goals further into even smaller steps such as making it to the next meal or to the next meeting, or even through the next hour or minute!

Activities such as meditation, regularly attending a support session, exercise and keeping yourself busy with hobbies can all help to distract you. Try to avoid places that will trigger a relapse or where you have identified barriers may occur.

SNAPSHOT

- Identify, Plan, Execute, Review – identify your goals, execute the plan, review your progress and put the work in to stay on track. You can achieve whatever you're prepared to achieve.
- Change your goals as you learn more about yourself – this is a journey, and nothing is absolute.
- Research suggests the more we track, the more we gain – if you know your starting point and end point, put a plan in place and track progress along the way, you're more likely to achieve your goals.
- Surround yourself with people who are supportive of what you're trying to achieve and will help you on your journey. You don't need people in your life who are dragging you down. Friends are supportive of each other.
- Once you've made your plan, only focus on the next smallest step. Sometimes considering the bigger picture for long periods of time can become overwhelming and demotivating. Your only goal in the moment is to achieve the next smallest step.
- Remember, health is wealth!

• Chapter 5 •

Managing Transition

Managing transition is understanding that, in everyday life, you will face barriers because of your gender identity and that isn't your fault. Society can be a hostile place for gender diverse people, with changes in law that affect life generally, as well as the media bombardment of trans communities and debates on trans lives and rights. All of this can take its toll on individuals. It's important to understand what might trigger a dip in your mental health and be able to take control, initiate self-care and keep moving forward towards your goals.

Recently we have seen debates around trans inclusion in sports, the consultation of the Gender Recognition Act, changes to the gender change service the government operates, debates on conversion therapy, as well as numerous related articles in mainstream media.

Managing symptoms of gender dysphoria and day-to-day barriers is crucial for reaching any goals you have set yourself in any other area of your life. Trans people face many barriers day to day that impact on mental health and emotional wellbeing; managing the impact this can have is essential to realising your full potential.

Waiting for any kind of treatment from NHS gender services currently is incredibly challenging and frustrating due to the long wait times for diagnosis and medical intervention. If you're looking to have hormone replacement therapy and top or bottom surgery, then unfortunately the wait time for this can be years. It's important that whilst you wait for medical intervention your mental health is the best it can be, enabling you to continue to reach other goals in your life and not get drawn into destructive behaviours. This will enable you to be in a strong position for the next step in your transition. As we saw in the previous chapter, physical health is just as important, so focusing on your wellbeing whilst you wait for medical intervention will ensure a smoother recovery from surgery with a higher chance of a positive outcome. Reframing your priorities to focusing on your wellbeing takes the spotlight off surgery and gives you something to occupy your mind, keeping you busy and focused on your goals, and has an overall positive impact on your life.

Daily barriers

For gender diverse communities, day-to-day life can be challenging, and when you're managing a busy life the issues that you might face daily can chip away at your self-esteem and confidence, throwing you off course from your personal goals.

It's important that binding, packing, tucking and other forms of gender affirmation strategies are done safely, to minimise risk of harm to the body. Gender affirmation strategies can be incredibly empowering for mental health and have an overall positive impact on mental health generally. However, if you're using gender affirmation strategies and are two years into a five-year wait for treatment, this can become tiresome over time and cause you to feel low and desperate. It's important that you listen to your body and take breaks from gender affirmation strategies whenever you can to lessen the impact. Some gender affirmation strategies cause permanent changes to the body, so to reduce impact, make sure you're implementing them safely. This will help in the long run when your time comes for surgery. You don't want to be dealing with a skin irritation/infection from binding or tucking, for example, if you're heading into the hospital for surgery. This might delay your surgery, which again will impact on mental health. However, gender affirmation strategies can help to reduce the feeling of gender dysphoria which can, at times, be crippling.

> **TOP TIP**
>
> Explore what works best for you to promote positive mental health and emotional wellbeing – be brave!

Other challenges that gender diverse communities can face are from members of the public. People are often misgendered and can face hostility in public places and sometimes even violence. The world can be a scary place sometimes, particularly if you're from a minority group.

If you're committed to reaching your personal goals, you will have to face the public to get there; there's no getting around that. So, let's look at how you can manage day-to-day life and keep striving towards reaching your personal goals.

The 4Ps model

One of the main strategies that you can use to identify and solve any problem is the 4Ps strategy. This has been used in business development for decades and was first used within marketing, developed initially in 1960 by E.J. McCarthy in his book *Basic Marketing: A Managerial Approach*. His model has been used to develop a similar model that we now use to tackle life's many issues and move forward to meet our goals.[1]

The 4Ps are:

+ Prep
+ Plan
+ Perform
+ Perfect

We'll use this strategy to help you overcome daily challenges and make long-lasting changes to your day-to-day life.

Prep

First, we'll consider the **prep** element of the model. Let's look at what challenges you are struggling with initially.

What are the main day-to-day barriers that you face?

....

....

....

....

....

....

If you could click your fingers and change this tomorrow, what would have changed?

....

....

....

....

....

....

Let's break this down into smaller steps. List one barrier you face:

....

....

---

1   https://medium.com/@MatHelme/the-four-ps-of-problem-solving-6e15a39a0712

....

....

Plan

Now that we understand the issue, we can **plan** to help you overcome these challenges. To make the most out of the 4Ps strategy, utilise other goal-planning/setting strategies such as the SMART acronym to help make sure your plan is realistic and achievable.

Let's take the barrier you've identified above. Write it down in the first column:

Column 1   Column 2   Column 3

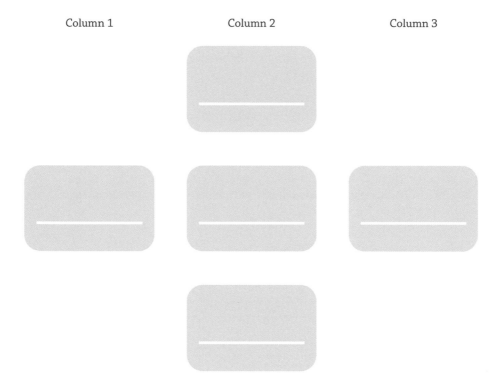

Now, in column 3, write down what you want your outcome to be. Column 2 represents the steps you're going to take to get to your ideal outcome in column 3. What's the missing piece to get you from column 1 to column 3? Here are some tips to help:

✦ If being misgendered is something that you struggle with daily, identify if you're being misgendered by someone at work or home or if it's members of the public. One solution you might be able to consider is challenging that person. You can plan and prepare for this. You want a positive outcome from any conversation whereby you're going to challenge someone about misgendering – if you're aggressive in tone when challenging people, they're likely to match their aggression to yours as they'll feel defensive. A sensitive, well-thought-out conversation that identities what the problem is and how it makes you feel, including the impact it has on you, is a possible solution to this problem. You can ask for help, from supportive people in your life, to plan out what you'd like to say. You should not feel the need to overcompensate for other people's behaviour but do consider there are ways of approaching conversations where you get the best outcome for you; using violence/aggression isn't one of them.

✦ If you're worried about being challenged in changing rooms at clothes shops, practise what you will say if you are challenged and how you might address this situation in real life. Use a friend to practise with or take a friend with you and agree a plan together so your friend can support you. If you're not ready to take on changing rooms and challenging people but still want to explore your identity and gender affirmation practice, try buying clothes online so you can try them on at home or in a safe space like a support group. Use a company that offers free returns/refunds so if you don't like your purchase, you can easily send it back.

Now you've identified the problem, the solution and the steps in between, it's time to plan for this to be executed.

Thinking about the steps in column 2, what do you need for this to happen? You might consider chatting to a friend to ask them for support with challenging something, or you might need to go back to the self-esteem and confidence chapter and set yourself a goal there to reach this goal. Identify what you need:

....

....

....

....

What do you currently have available that will help you obtain what you need?

....

....

Who or what can help you obtain what you need?

....

....

Reminder: is it SMART? If not, review what you've written and identify what needs to change to make it SMART.

Being prepared for big changes in your life is important in ensuring that you stay on track with your goals. We can't predict the future, so identifying all possible outcomes to a scenario, and therefore preparing what you might do if each one occurs, can help you to be prepared and not waver from what you're trying to achieve longer term.

Thinking about the steps you've planned to take to address the problem, what are all the possible outcomes?

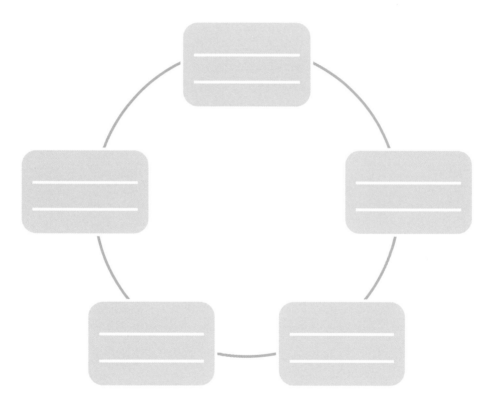

For each of the potential outcomes, find a possible solution that is realistic and that will enable you to challenge what happens and support you towards getting your preferred outcome:

....

....

....

....

....

....

....

....

....

....

....

....

As we've seen in the previous chapters, all the models we've used include a degree of preparation; it's essential to achieving your full potential. For example, delivering a presentation without preparing it first is a recipe for disaster; you need to plan it first, do a practice run, change things as you go along and then deliver the final package. That way you'll get the best outcome – the same is true for achieving your personal goals.

Perform

Congratulations – you've identified the first two steps on your way towards your preferred future. The next step of the 4Ps model is **perform**.

The perform element of the model means it's time for action. Following on from the last step where you've identified what you need to help you take the first step, it's now time to do it!

So...what's the first smallest step?

....

....

Identify what your next steps are here to meet your goal:

....

....

....

....

....

....

Think about when you would like to reach your first goal, then work backwards from this to understand at what point you want to act and make progress towards it. When do you want to have achieved your goal? What is the timeframe?

....

....

....

....

Working backways from your overall goal, when will you execute the first step of your plan to ensure you reach the final outcome in time?

....

....

Once you've done the first step, when will the next steps need to happen to keep on track to achieving your goal?

....

....

....

....

....

....

How will you know that you have achieved your goal? What evidence will there be?

....

....

....

....

....

....

TOP TIP
Fail to prepare, prepare to fail.

Perfect

The final step of this model is **perfect**. You might not reach your desired outcome first time round, but there's no such as thing as failure; there are only opportunities to learn. Reframing 'failure' will help you in this section; understanding that 'failure' is an essential part of any learning process is key.

Fear of failure often holds people back, but no one usually gets everything right first-time round, and if you're not prepared to reframe 'failure' as an essential part of moving towards your preferred future, you'll become demotivated and struggle to learn what you need to learn in order to overcome the barrier you're facing.

You've executed your plans and now you'll have the outcome of the problem you faced. Reflecting on the outcome, think about the following.

What went well?

....

....

....

....

....

....

What have you learnt about yourself from moving through this process and tackling your problem?

....

....

....

....

....

....

How do you feel now having worked towards or achieved your goal?

....

....

....

....

What did you achieve?

....

....

....

....

Did you get the desired outcome? Was it better or worse than you expected?

....

....

....

....

Reviewing the progress you have made, what have you learnt that could make this process easier next time?

....

....

....

....

....

....

If you didn't get the desired outcome, revisit your plan, identify where things went wrong and change it. With this in mind, answer the following questions.

What do you need to change?

....

....

....

....

When will you do this by?

....

What outcome do you want this time round?

....

....

....

....

What will you say to yourself if things don't go to plan? Ensure this is based on positive affirmations rather than limiting beliefs – be your own best friend!

....

....

....

....

What do you know about yourself already that will enable you to push forward and try again?

....

....

....

....

Sometimes there isn't a straightforward solution to a problem you might be facing, but we always have a choice in respect of changing our perspectives. Our perspectives can be reframed so we can find a different way to look at a situation. This can take some time, work and practice. Practising reframing strategies can help in all areas of your life, alleviating stress and helping you to see the world from a new perspective. Changing your perspective can also help you to find solutions you might not have ordinarily considered, for example by chatting the situation through with a friend.

A good example of this is reframing surgery waiting times to thinking of this as an opportunity to review your personal goals, try new things, find yourself, gain new experiences, learn new skills or get fitter and healthier so you're ready for surgery. Whilst that's not intended to diminish the difficulties that people face with waiting for medical treatment, it's important to recognise that reframing this can help open your mind up to new opportunities and possibilities. Focusing on other areas of your life and striving for a goal off your bucket list, for example, shifts the focus onto something other than waiting lists. We have no control over the waiting lists for surgical treatment and the longer people wait for surgery the bigger the impact this has on overall wellbeing. Finding something to focus on that you are interested in or that supports your preferred future can help to mitigate the strain waiting lists puts on gender diverse communities.

> **TOP TIP**
>
> Focus on what you can do and change, and not what you can't.

Managing transition daily can be an incredibly challenging task in itself, but as we've seen above using the 4Ps model, if we plan and are prepared we can overcome anything. Self-care is an essential strategy to be able to meet your basic needs every day, enabling you to thrive in other areas of your life. Having a good self-care routine that is well practised over time can help you keep your head above the water even on the darkest of days. Here are some tips to help you embed a self-care routine that works for you:

- ✦ Make a morning routine and stick to it.
- ✦ Pick a time to get up every morning and put this into practice.
- ✦ Set yourself one task that will move you towards any of your goals each day. It doesn't matter how small this task is; if it's achievable and you complete it, you'll feel a sense of purpose and be more motivated to carry on moving towards your preferred future.
- ✦ Meet every self-care task with commitment – set your intentions to do everything to the best of your ability. Practising this will help reframe your mind as well as ensuring you're reaching your full potential.
- ✦ Ensure your self-care routine includes breaks from things like binding, packing and tucking to enable your body to repair, keeping you fit, healthy and performing at your best.
- ✦ Rest is essential to progress, burnout is real! Incorporate rest days, social activities and fun!
- ✦ Think about some treats to indulge yourself a little – treat yourself to these once you've reached milestones. This can help with motivation as you'll have something to strive for and look forward to.

If you struggle with meeting your basic needs, then your self-care routine is essential. It's okay to have to revisit your self-care routine and strategies and scale back achieving your personal goals; it means you're repairing and preparing to move forward and reach them.

Your self-care routine should be manageable – trying to incorporate many different positive things in your life as well as managing busy jobs and family can be a challenge. You don't need to pack your schedule with activities and self-promises if this is going to make your life more stressful; it's counterproductive. Commit to a few daily practices that will promote wellbeing and push you forward rather than hold you back.

Self-care routine

Let's look at the basics: here we're considering the absolute minimum you need to do to maintain your day-to-day life (see also the section on self-care in Chapter 4). Good examples include proper nutrition, exercise, being hydrated, getting a good night's sleep and refraining from drugs, alcohol or destructive behaviours. It seems a lot when you read that back but if you commit yourself to a good self-care routine, you're building the foundations for your future and this will help you perform exceptionally when you need to nail that presentation for work, hit a deadline or achieve something you've worked towards.

What do you need to maintain good health and wellbeing daily? Examples include showering, a good morning routine (e.g. eating breakfast, brushing your teeth, setting yourself a time to get up every day), incorporating exercise into your daily routine and drinking 2 litres of water a day. What does this look like for you? Pick four to five self-care activities that you will commit to:

1. ....
2. ....
3. ....
4. ....
5. ....

If you do each of these things every day for three months, what will the benefits for you be?

....
....
....
....
....
....

On a scale of 1 to 10, 1 being not important, 10 being essential, how important are these tasks to you?

(1) (2) (3) (4) (5) (6) (7) (8) (9) (10)

On a scale of 1 to 10, 1 being not committed, 10 being fully committed, how committed are you to completing these tasks?

(1) (2) (3) (4) (5) (6) (7) (8) (9) (10)

If you're not fully committed to completing your daily tasks, what is holding you back? What needs to happen for you to move up one more point on the scale and make a commitment to yourself and your future?

....

....

....

....

Breaking this down into smaller steps, what do you need to do to make this happen?

....

....

....

....

....

....

Self-care requires some degree of effort and commitment on your part. If you're struggling to complete everyday tasks, take one or two things off your list and commit to a smaller list, or break down these steps further into manageable steps. Committing to your self-care steps for one week isn't going to give you life-changing results – change takes time, commitment, dedication and effort – so make sure your steps and tasks are manageable. Once you feel like you've achieved those one or two tasks that you committed to over a few months, you might be in a better place emotionally to take on an extra step. You're looking to initially take the smallest step, because it doesn't matter how small a step it is that you're taking, it's about moving forward and progressing – whatever that looks like for you.

Self-care is a very personal endeavour; one person's self-care routine might be very different to others', and they may have built this up over time. Don't compare yourself or your progress with other people's. This is a personal journey and there's only one perspective that matters – yours!

5 steps for mental wellbeing

The 5 steps to mental wellbeing as advised by the NHS is a great tool to use if you need some additional support with building your self-care and wellbeing plans.[2] The programme focuses on five key areas of your life that, when implemented, can help you stay healthy, get back on track and reach your goals.

Step 1 – connect with others

Connecting with others is vital to our emotional health and wellbeing. We are social beings and it's important that we connect with others to bring a sense of belonging and community to our worlds.

Who do you have in your life that you enjoy spending time with?

....
....
....
....
....
....

Why are they important to you?

....
....
....
....
....
....

---

2   www.nhs.uk/mental-health/self-help/guides-tools-and-activities/five-steps-to-mental-wellbeing

Set aside some time each week to connect with these people. It could be a set phone call or double up the wellbeing points by taking a walk with them or sharing a meal. How will you incorporate spending time with people into your week? Remember to make sure that this is achievable and realistic:

....

....

....

....

....

....

If you don't feel you have people in your life that you can connect with, what can you do to build some new relationships? Is it time to start a new class? Have you got a hobby or skill you can share with others by volunteering? Have you been meaning to start a new exercise group? You could even consider joining a social group or book club. What can you do to build relationships?

....

....

....

....

....

....

> **TOP TIP**
>
> We're living in a time when video calling is now much more accessible than it used to be. This is a good opportunity to meet with people, especially if they live far away from you, but don't let this replace meaningful face-to-face connection.

Step 2 – be physically active
Physical exercise is essential to everyone's wellbeing. Exercise releases endorphins into the brain which alleviate stress and anxiety and help us to function at our best and think more clearly.

Are there any exercises that you enjoy doing? Did you exercise as a child? Have you been meaning to get back into a sport or activity but have struggled?

....

....

....

....

What is the first, smallest step you can take to getting back into exercise or stepping things up to the next level?

....

....

....

....

You could consider finding out about local classes or sports teams, speaking to a trainer or researching gym prices. You can find plenty of exercise videos on YouTube, and the NHS website has some great examples of incorporating exercise into your daily life.

What benefits will you see from exercising?

....

....

....

....

....

....

Why is this important to your day-to-day wellbeing?

....

....

....

....

....

....

Do you need some motivation? Think about signing up to an event for charity or working out with a friend who might want to try something new as well. You could even commit to starting that couch to 5K app that you've been meaning to get to.

Exercise doesn't need to be costly, and you don't need to sign up to Iron Man (unless you want to!), but having a goal like a sponsored run/cycle/swim can help motivate you to turn up each day, write a training plan and most importantly – stick to it! Start small and build on your exercise goals over time.

What do you want to achieve from exercising?

....

....

....

....

What steps do you need to take to reach your goal?

....

....

....

....

When will you start?

....

How will you know you've achieved your goal? What evidence will you see of your progress?

....

....

....

....

....

....

What will it mean to you when you've achieved what you set out to?

....

....

....

....

Step 3 – learn new skills

Learning is an essential part of life and any goal-setting journey you embark on. Learning will help you achieve your goals. If you don't hit your targets first time round, you should always reflect and learn on what went well and what you can improve on. Then you try again, putting into practice what you have learnt. Lifelong learning is what makes life interesting, and your ability to learn and continue to grow and develop will enable you to try new experiences and achieve personal goals that you can't even imagine right now. It also sets an example to others around you, that you can achieve whatever you put your mind to.

If you struggle with your mental health generally, learning new techniques or skills to manage this will help. You can use self-help books available in libraries or learn via YouTube or by downloading PDF documents, for example. It doesn't matter how you learn; it's what you learn that counts. If you're challenging yourself to do something new as part of working through this book, then researching and learning about your chosen task will help you in the long run.

What do you want to learn?

....

....

Why do you want to learn this?

....

....

....

....

How will this new knowledge benefit you? How will this help you achieve your goals?

....

....

....

....

Is there a skill you've been wanting to learn or develop further? What is it?

....

....

What will this new skill bring to your life?

....

....

....

....

How will your learning journey support your mental health and emotional wellbeing?

....

....

....

....

You can choose to learn anything, and it doesn't need to be something that will help you achieve your goals directly. Learning in general can help you reach new levels of personal awareness and understanding of the world, which helps to change perspectives and build confidence.

Here are some top tips to get you started on your learning journey:

- Choose something you want to learn or develop, something that interests you.
- Use resources such as books, audio books, the library, YouTube, online courses or even night classes at your local college – pick something that suits you and your lifestyle.
- Incorporate learning into your day-to-day life – get up half an hour earlier, listen to an audio book on your commute, read a book for half an hour before you go to sleep.
- Reflect on what you've learnt and how you feel each day by keeping a diary – you don't have to write huge amounts, just a few bullet points to help you embed your learning will suffice.

Step 4 – give to others

Giving to others is an incredible way to build relationships, give back to your communities and learn. Giving helps to create positive feelings and emotions for you as well as helping to give a sense of purpose and belonging. Volunteering is a great way to give back to your community and has many benefits. Supporting local charities, building relationships with others and making new friends is emotionally rewarding. You don't have to give hours and hours of your time or resources; you could give your time online or donate something to someone in need.

Think about something that you're good at or that you enjoy or even something you feel passionately about. We've all got something in our lives that we've been affected by and that's made us passionate about causes. Choosing something that means something to you is an important first step if you are ready to volunteer and give back.

What is important to you in relation to helping others/giving back? This could be a charity, a cause or even supporting someone you care about:

....
....
....
....

What do you want to share with others?

....
....
....
....

How will this help the communities or people you're supporting?

....
....
....
....

What will the sharing of your skills or time bring to your life? What benefits can you expect?

....
....

....

....

What's the first smallest step to making this happen?

....

....

If you do have a charity in mind, this could be about getting in touch with them; if you don't, your first step could be to find out about opportunities to volunteer. This could also be less 'official'. Maybe you have an elderly neighbour who's alone who might appreciate someone to have a cup of tea with every now and again. Whatever it is, make sure it means something to you.

Build this into your life. You could volunteer once a year or once a week; it's entirely up to you; giving back gives you a sense of meaning and purpose and will bring something special to your life.

Step 5 – be in the moment

One of the biggest life skills that you can learn is to live in the moment. Being present in every moment helps to give a sense of life and enables you to live all your life experiences to their fullest. Mindfulness has become popular over the last few years since the push for mental health awareness has grown. Mindfulness or awareness is about paying attention to everything that you do including even the most mundane of tasks. Being aware is about focusing on what you're doing (or not doing) all the time. According to the NHS and National Institute for Care Excellence, meditation is recommended as a treatment for depression.[3] Being present can help us recognise our thoughts and feelings, slow down the world and help to alleviate symptoms of stress.

Practising mindfulness every day can help to promote self-discipline and positive mental health, which will help you achieve your longer-term goals and support you to enjoy the process of achievement too.

There are lots of apps out there, both free and to buy, and also videos on YouTube that you can use as resources to start you on your mindfulness journey. However, practising mindfulness is something that you can do every day, without resources, just by clearing your mind and focusing on the tasks that you are doing. Quietening the mind can help you think more clearly, problem solve easily and help you feel more relaxed daily.

---

3   https://www.nhs.uk/mental-health/self-help/tips-and-support/mindfulness

What do you need to do to start your mindfulness journey? You can incorporate this goal into your learning goal:

....

....

What is the first smallest step?

....

....

When will you start?

....

....

What benefits will mindfulness have on your wellbeing?

....

....

....

....

How will you know you're becoming more mindful? What evidence will you see?

....

....

....

....

Mindfulness is a skill and therefore something that needs to be practised daily.

Emergency planning

We must acknowledge that as part of being human, some days feel a lot worse than others. It's important that we can recognise when these days are happening so we can be proactive in recovering, move back to the daily self-care tasks and get back on track to reaching our goals.

Emergency safety or wellbeing planning is essential to helping you stay safe during difficult times and to help manage your wellbeing. Earlier we considered the 4Ps approach to goal setting, with planning being an essential part of that.

Having an emergency wellbeing plan can help you feel more secure in that you've got a plan to fall back on if you're really struggling. Emergency planning also helps you to feel more in control if you are facing a difficult time and enables you to reach out for support, recover and get back on track to reaching your personal goals.

It's essential you understand that an emergency plan is an important step to reaching your goals; it's not a plan when all else fails, it's not a plan when you've not achieved what you wanted to achieve – it's a plan to help you to continue to grow, manage your wellbeing and succeed with your goals.

How will you know that you need to start using your emergency plan? What will you feel? What might other people see or hear that would suggest you might need to use your emergency plan?

....

....

....

....

....

....

Who can you reach out to for support?

....

....

....

....

What can these people do to support you?

....

....

....

....

....

....

Do you have any triggers that might mean you need to use your emergency plan?

....

....

....

....

....

....

Can these triggers be prevented? If so, how?

....

....

....

....

....

....

What is going to keep you safe in the moment? Consider getting rid of anything that might cause you harm, going to a safe place, speaking to someone who cares about you or using a helpline:

....

....

....

....

....

....

What helps you to feel better? Think about food you like to cook, eat or buy; activities that make you feel good like watching your favourite TV show; being creative; listening to music; exercising:

....

....

....

....

....

....

What do you have in your life that is important to you? Think about friends, family, pets, your career, your transition:

....

....

....

....

....

....

What are your hopes for the future? What are you looking forward to that will help you through this difficult time?

....

....

....

....

....

....

What resources do you need to make sure your emergency plan is always accessible? Consider creative resources, books, mental health tools, phone or text numbers for helplines or services. List them here:

....

....

....

....

....

....

Make these resources accessible. If you haven't already done so, you can create a box of your resources so that when you start using your emergency plan all you'll need to do is reach for your box and find what you need. Sometimes when people feel low, they find it difficult to think clearly, so having everything to hand in one place can really help ease the pressure of trying to remember everything in your plan. In your box, add things that represent whatever is important to you; this could be photos of people or pictures from a vision board that give you hope for the future. A reminder of what you're trying to achieve will help you to focus on your future and will help distract you. Distraction techniques can be incredibly useful, so include a list of these in your box:

+ Counting things around you, for example how many blue items can you see?
+ Concentrating on the moment – how many things can you see, what can you hear, smell and touch?
+ Doodling or colouring – adult colouring books are readily available at a reasonable price.
+ Focusing on your breathing only or practising mindfulness techniques.
+ Imagining a safe place or a place in your life that you have been to that invokes positive memories.
+ Exercise.
+ Being in nature.
+ Listening to a podcast (there are plenty of free podcasts available on a variety of subjects on most smart phones).
+ Singing.
+ Watching your favourite film – or pick an inspirational film that you enjoy that can help motivate you to continue your journey.
+ Playing a game.
+ Speaking to a friend.
+ Reading a book.

Add any other distraction techniques for your box here:

....

....

....

....

....

....

Now find yourself an old shoe box and put everything you need in there. That way you'll have a backup plan if you find you are struggling with your mental health and wellbeing.

SNAPSHOT

- 📷 Plan, prepare, execute and perfect – use this model to manage your day-to-day transition and your transition goals. Having a clear focus and plans in place helps to manage mental health daily and prevents crisis.
- 📷 Role play challenging situations – this will help you feel confident if you need to use your strategies in the wider world.
- 📷 Implement your self-care plan. You can write plans for the rest of your life, but they won't be any use to you if you don't implement them.
- 📷 Take the next smallest step and only focus on that step. Sometimes you can get overwhelmed when you are constantly looking at the bigger picture. All you need to do is focus on the next step. When you put all the small steps you've taken together, that's when you'll see your goals realised.
- 📷 Take time for yourself to recover, relax and enjoy day-to-day life. Implement the strategies you've learnt. You might find some strategies work better than others – you don't need to do all the strategies all the time.
- 📷 Emergency planning is a great way to support your mental health and well-being – it's an act of self-care in and of itself that, when implemented, will help you to recover and look after yourself when you need it the most.

Chapter 6

Relationships

As a human you are naturally a social being. Relationships are a key part of the human experience for all walks of life at any age, and they can have both a positive and negative effect on our lives. The relationships that we have can be the difference between going for that next opportunity we've wanted for such a long time or not. Relationships can help you when you need a bit of extra care or a shoulder to cry on, but they can sometimes make things worse. Many people believe that they find out who their real friends and family are by coming out and going through the process of transitioning. For many, seeing who stands by your side when things get tough can strengthen and give meaning to relationships. For others, it can mean relationships that they valued and respected coming to an end.

Relationships can take many forms, from intense friendships to acquaintances, romantic partners and colleagues as well as parent–child relationships. Every relationship is different and each relationship you have with someone will bring something different to your life. Sometimes relationships can be unbalanced and have a negative impact on your life. In this chapter we'll explore how to cultivate positive and healthy relationships, improve the ones you want to improve, and cut out the people who do not align themselves with your values and vision for the future.

Our relationships can bring immense joy to our lives; other people's kindness and giving to others ourselves both bring emotional rewards that cannot be replicated or bought. They can also bring heartache when losing someone or impact upon our confidence and self-esteem. It's the nature of relationships that can determine whether people reach their full potential. Analysing the relationships in your life and understanding the impact that each of them has on your life can bring you a greater understanding of the benefits and drawbacks of your relationships, how you can improve them or leave them behind, as well as gaining deeper insight into the impact on your mental health and emotional wellbeing. The better you know yourself as a person, the more you can bring to your relationships that benefits both you and those around you.

Identity and relationships

Bringing your authentic self to relationships is what helps to make them balanced and encourages you to feel safe as well as supporting you to build effective relationships. Relationships where you don't feel safe to express yourself or bring your whole identity can lead to feelings of insecurity, worry and stress, all of which have a negative impact on your wellbeing. Bringing your identity to the forefront of your relationships can also mean you experience a sense of freedom to share your experiences, thoughts and feelings and are not held back by worrying about outing yourself. This can enhance relationships as others learn more about you and can encourage people to support you on your lifelong learning journey.

Living authentically is a term that is thrown around a lot within transgender communities and most believe that it is related to being out loud and proud. However, living authentically is a personal concept; it's about what is authentic to you: what your identity means to you personally. Everyone experiences their identity differently, physically, emotionally and socially, so authenticity comes from a deep sense of personal experience and reflection on what your identity means to you.

What does living authentically mean for you? How does this manifest itself in your everyday life?

....

....

....

....

....

....

Encourage yourself to live authentically in the way that suits you and only you.

For the purposes of these next exercises, we'll focus on decisions around either living stealth or coming out and the impact on relationships.

Some people choose to live their lives stealth as trans people, and others are out loud and proud or somewhere in between the two. However you decide to present your identity is a personal choice, and no one should be pushed into either being out or living stealth; it is a personal decision. It's important to recognise that being out and living stealth can both come with their own risks and can impact the relationships you have with others. Making the decision to be out or live stealth is a big decision and should be made by putting in some time to reflect on what matters most to you and what you want to bring to the lives of others. You will then be able to make a more informed decision.

It's important to understand how you can bring your authentic self to your relationships no matter how you present your identity within them. Relationships, particularly romantic ones, can cause you to worry, especially about what your new or potential lifelong partner might think of your identity and what you might stand to gain or lose because of sharing that within your relationships. Use the exercises here to reflect on any relationship in which you're considering either living stealth or coming out and how to decide that's right for you. (If you feel you don't need to work through this section, then skip to the values section of this chapter.)

The most important question you need to ask yourself if you are in this situation is: what do you want from your relationships?

....
....
....
....
....
....

Thinking about what you have written here, do you think being 'out' or 'living stealth' is crucial to you being able to gain what you need from these relationships?

....
....
....
....

Think about your answer. If you were to be out or live stealth within this relationship, what would you gain from both perspectives?

....
....
....
....
....
....

Thinking about your answer again, if you were to be out or live stealth within this relationship, what do you feel you might lose that is important to you?

....

....

....

....

....

....

Understanding risks and assessing against them is key to help you make decisions about anything in your life, not just your relationships. Understanding what you might be set to gain or lose from any particular situation, mitigating the potential risk of loss and then making your decision can help ensure you make informed decisions that are right for you.

Are there any opportunities for you to gain further knowledge or insight on how another person might react to you coming out or to finding out you're living stealth?

....

....

....

....

You could consider watching a documentary about trans issues with this person or commenting about a book you might have read recently to start a conversation. This may help you to understand how that person feels about trans communities and identities and therefore help you make an informed decision.

What opportunities do you have to find out further information that will help you decide on your next step?

....

....

....

....

When will you do this by?

....

Review

What have you learnt from completing the above actions that you set yourself?

....

....

....

....

....

....

Do you feel you have enough information to make an informed decision?

....

If not, are there any further opportunities you have, to find out more information? If so, what are they?

....

....

....

....

When will you do this by?

....

Reflecting on the information you now have, are you leaning more towards coming out or continuing to live stealth?

....

Why?

....

....

....

What points do you want to get across to this person? Use bullet points to plan this:

....

....

....

....

....

....

Using bullet points can help you to remember the points you want to get across. Keeping it short and to the point enables you to express what you need without missing anything out that you might feel is crucial to moving forward.

When will you do this by?

....

On a scale of 1 to 10, 1 being not at all confident, 10 being the most confident, how confident do you feel in executing your plan?

(1) (2) (3) (4) (5) (6) (7) (8) (9) (10)

Is there anyone in your life that could support you in making this decision or support you with speaking to the person you want to speak to? Who is this?

....

How can you approach them for help? You don't always have to speak directly to someone to connect with them. You could use letter writing, email, text messaging, voice notes or invite them over for a coffee to chat. What will you do?

....

....

When will you do this by?

....

Plan what you want to say here using short bullet points:

....

....

....

....

....

....

When will you do this by?

....

What was the outcome?

....

....

....

....

Contingency plan

Things don't always go to plan, even with the best of preparations. It's important to mitigate the damage when things don't go the way in which you envisaged.

Think about the worst-case scenario from the decision you have made. What could happen?

....

....

....

....

This exercise is designed to help and support you when you don't get the outcome that you want; it is not designed to cause further worry or stress. It's okay to decide against your original plan to either come out or remain stealth in your relationships; you can revisit this when the time is right. Choosing the right time to execute plans for anything in your life can help support a positive outcome.

Back to your contingency plan. How would you feel if your worst-case scenario occurred?

....

....

....

....

Who can you reach out to for support if this happens?

....

....

What do you think you will need from them?

....

....

....

....

Communicating what you need from your support networks if your worst-case scenario does happen can help you to recover and move forward. This is because when you are overcome by emotions it can be challenging to think logically about what helps you to feel better. Having a plan so the people around you know what to do can help you heal; they will be armed with your personal strategies that they can remind you of when you are struggling.

When making decisions in your life that affect the trajectory of your relationships, it can feel incredibly daunting, and your mind can feel like it is going round in a vicious circle. By thinking about it, writing down concerns, planning and having a contingency plan, you're giving yourself the time and space to think more clearly, find solutions and make the right decisions for you.

Values

Building relationships might seem straightforward to some people, but for others it takes a bit more of a strategic approach and some reflection time to understand what helps them to build relationships and what draws them to certain people over others. Sometimes people are also put in positions where they are forced to have some sort of civil or working relationship with others who they might not necessarily choose to spend time with but still need to work with, for example. These are the relationships that may seem harder to build on, but the strategies and activities in this section will help with this and put you in a better position to improve other skills such as teamwork, communication, negotiation and compromise. For any relationship to flourish, a strong foundation is required.

In the personal values section at the start of this book, you identified the values that you felt represented you and how you wanted to live your life in accordance with those. Now let's consider the values that you respect and feel are important to you in others.

Reflect on a time when you've been positively influenced or affected by someone else's behaviour or experience that directly impacted you. What happened?

....
....
....
....
....

How did you feel following your interactions with this person? What impact did they have on you?

....
....
....
....

What traits or behaviours did the other person display?

....
....
....
....

If you need some help with this question, think about the following terms that might help best describe behaviours/value-based responses:

Compassion	Kindness	Generosity	Respect	Passion
Leadership	Bravery	Wisdom	Honesty	Loyalty
Authenticity	Genuineness	Altruism	Consideration	Sincerity

Why were that person's actions so important to you?

....
....
....
....
....
....

Did this impact the relationship that you had/have with this person?

....

If so, how?

....

....

....

....

Are there any other traits or characteristics that you feel are essential for you to build a relationship with someone? List them here:

....

....

....

....

There are some relationships that are easier to manage than others and some where you meet someone, seem to hit it off straight away and wonder where that person has been all your life. Other relationships take a little longer to develop, and sometimes you must make the effort to find some common ground for you both to then move forward and get what you need from each other, particularly if that is within a work/education capacity, where you don't have the ability to choose your teacher or your boss, for example.

Finding common ground with someone can be a great way to start implementing a foundation to your relationship with them., This helps you both to see that you might have more in common than you do differences. This can be difficult when you are building a relationship where your fundamental values clash. Nonetheless, you will still have something you can discuss – even if it's a work project! This can also help when you're trying to repair a relationship or where there might be conflict.

Think about a relationship you have with someone that you feel needs to be improved. What is the issue?

....

....

....

....

....

....

Breaking it down into smaller steps, how did you get to where you are with this person now?

....

....

....

....

....

....

Can you pinpoint a particular time when your relationship with this person started to deteriorate?

....

....

....

....

Reflecting on your own behaviour, was there anything you feel you could have done or said differently?

....

....

....

....

Are there any opportunities for you to share this insight with the person?

....

....

....

If so, when will you do this by?

....

Sharing your reflections on behaviour that might have impacted or contributed to a negative relationship is a great way to put your relationship back on the right track. It doesn't necessarily mean you'll become the best of friends, but it does mean you've got a starting point to build upon. Being able to share insights into your own conduct enables relationships to repair – after all, you're only human and everyone makes mistakes. Having the ability to admit that can take a lot of emotional stamina, but it can also relieve pressure and stress in trying to defend yourself even thought there might have been things you said that could have exacerbated the issue. You can only take responsibility for your actions, not someone else's – that is their responsibility.

A great way in which you can start this process is by planning what you want to say. The aim here is to *repair* the relationship; this exercise is not intended to make you, or the other person, feel shame or humiliation about the behaviour that caused the issue initially.

Considering this exercise from the perspective that you want to *repair* the relationship, what would you say to the person you're addressing? Remember – you can only control and reflect on your own behaviour, and emphasising that may help the other person to reflect on their behaviour and reciprocate similarly towards you. Plan what you'd like to say below: think about three key points you'd like to raise (don't worry if there aren't as many as that); by focusing on a few points you'll make it easier to remember what you want to say in the moment, and you'll feel more in control of how you want your points to come across, as well as ensuring you don't miss anything out:

....

....

....

....

....

....

....

....

....

....

....

Now, practise, practise, practise. Knowing what you want to say and how you want this to come across can help you control your emotions in the moment when things may become heated.

When is the next available opportunity to have this discussion?

....

If there isn't an opportunity, how can you cultivate one? Is there an appropriate moment you can think of when you can ask this person if you can chat to them? Identify it here:

....

....

If you'd feel more comfortable having a third person there to mediate, then ask someone that is neutral to both parties if they are happy to facilitate a conversation – this should be consented to by the other person also.

Your intentions for this conversation will shape the outcome. If you are intending on making the relationship better, it's more likely that you'll come out of the conversation with a positive outcome because that's what you will be working towards. If your intentions are to put up a fight, your emotions going into the conversation will be heightened and this will come out in your body language, mannerisms and the way you use your words. Identifying what outcome you want from the situation can help you to work towards that. Ensure the outcome you want will positively impact your future relationship.

What outcome do you want following this conversation?

....

....

....

....

....

....

A positive strategy to obtain the outcome you want is to verbalise this to the person you're addressing. This also makes way for the other person to tell you what they would like the outcome to be, which you can then both work towards. Identifying the outcome you want uses similar principles to that of goal setting

– identify the goal, plan, take the next smallest steps, overcome the barriers, reach the goal and reap the reward. You don't have to be best friends with everyone, but there are some relationships that require a civil or working relationship which can be mutually beneficial in the long run, especially if you both have shared goals at work/school.

Sharing your insights with others can also help the other person to reflect on their own behaviour, and the process of sharing your thoughts and feelings about your own behaviour opens the door for the other person to do the same. You can't change someone else's behaviour or control other people, but what you can do is take responsibility for yourself and learn from your mistakes. Role modelling behaviour like this also gives permission for others to be vulnerable, and when the other party shares how they feel about their behaviour, this can enable you to move past the issue and start to re-build.

Strengths

Having a better understanding of your strengths in relationships can help you build on these, use them to your advantage, and cultivate positive, healthy and strong relationships that work for all parties.

To get you thinking about your relationships and strengths, let's start with relationships that don't require any maintenance. Think about someone in your life, a person that you don't see for a long time who you can still speak to and it feels like you've never been apart. A relationship where it feels like nothing has changed between you, despite your lives going separate ways, but when you do connect with them again the spark of your relationship is still very much alive, and it feels like you're the best of friends all over again!

What do you think are the traits that make the relationship with this person work? Consider things like mutual values, for example. Write down what makes this relationship work despite you having to spend little time maintaining it:

....

....

....

....

....

....

From this list, is there anything you feel particularly stands out? Is there anything here that you can focus on as being a key element that supports the relationship, and something you can use as a strategy to apply to other relationships in your life?

....

....

....

....

....

....

Why is this important to you?

....

....

....

....

....

....

What is your contribution to this relationship that makes it special and different from others?

....

....

....

....

....

Use your reflections here as a foundation for this chapter. Try to implement what you have learnt and apply it to other exercises. Use this if you feel the traits in this relationship are crucial to success in others.

Personal strengths

It can be difficult to try to identify your strengths on your own; often people can struggle with finding positive qualities to identify about themselves, so this exercise is based on using someone's else's insights to support you in identifying what strengths you do have.

Think about a person that you trust and whose opinion you value – someone that you have a strong relationship with. Who is this person?

....

Ask them what they think your strengths within relationships are. To help support you with this, try asking some of the following questions:

- ✦ What makes our relationship strong?
- ✦ What strengths do you think I bring to this relationship?
- ✦ What is my best quality in a relationship?
- ✦ What do you think promotes healthy relationships?

Some topics for discussion could include communication skills, listening skills, the ability to empathise, the ability to show support, being understanding of situations, providing advice and guidance, and being able to sensitively approach difficult subjects and say things to others that they might need to hear, but that are challenging to say.

Write the feedback you get from this person here:

....
....
....
....
....
....

Do you agree with what this person has said?

....

Are there any strengths that this person didn't say that you feel you also have? Write them down here:

....
....
....
....
....

Of the list of strengths you have identified, which of these qualities stand out as being the most important to you? Reflect on the values you've identified in earlier chapters to support you:

....

....

....

....

Knowing what your strengths are within relationships and having them at the forefront of your mind when interacting with others, building new relationships or repairing relationships will support you to ensure you're leading with your strengths and therefore providing more opportunities for positive interactions with others.

Now comes the more challenging part: reflecting on what you would like to improve or challenges you have had that impact on your relationships. We'll start with self-reflection before moving on to asking a trusted person in your life for feedback.

Reflect on the relationships in your life already. Think about a relationship that might need to be improved, for example. What do you see as your weaknesses within that relationship?

....

....

....

....

It can be easy to blame others for their shortcomings and for the reasons why relationships aren't working. Disagreeing with someone is normal and healthy; however, with disagreement there must also be acceptance. Accepting that someone else has a different opinion to yours enables relationships to continue without having a detrimental impact on both parties. Understanding this and putting this into practice, trying to empathise and understand the situation from their perspective, can help you to move forward together. This doesn't mean you have to maintain a relationship where your fundamental values clash on serious issues, this is around addressing minor issues and continuing to build relationships.

Of the weaknesses listed above that you would like to improve, are there any that you feel are most important or that you would like to prioritise? Are there any skills or attributes you would like to develop?

....

....

....

....

If you're struggling with identifying a skill or attribute you would like to develop, you could consider reflecting on the following, identifying something on the list:

+ Accepting and celebrating difference.
+ Listening skills.
+ Time efficiency – giving people more of your time.
+ Communication skills.
+ Learning to trust others.
+ Developing empathy.
+ Managing conflict better.
+ Committing to relationships that are important to you.

Many of the items on the list above are excellent skills to continue to develop throughout your life. Even if some of these are on your list of strengths, you can always make improvements with the things you are good at already!

Having reflected on what you would like to improve, how do you feel?

....

....

....

....

Sometimes we can feel a sense of power and control when assessing things in our life we want to develop or improve upon, and sometimes we can feel negative about the fact that there are things to improve. Don't let this exercise be an excuse to beat yourself up; the point of this is for you to develop skills and a deeper understanding of who you are as a person and how to become the best version of yourself. Learning is part of the process.

Think about a person you have a strong relationship with and who you trust. Ask them for their feedback on what they think you can improve upon in relationships. Here are some questions to help prompt the person you are asking:

+ What do you think I can improve on within relationships?

✦ Has there ever been a time when you have been upset by my actions or behaviours? If so, what was the issue? (Focus on skill development and not criticising the person or using this as an opportunity to open old wounds.)
✦ What is the most important strength in a relationship? Is this something that I already possess, or should I look to improve this?
✦ Are there any situations you have observed when I've interacted with others where you thought I could have handled the situation differently? If so, what happened and what advice would you give me for next time?

How do you feel about the feedback you have received?

....
....
....
....

TOP TIP

Remember! We're using this as an opportunity to develop, not to criticise or undermine you. You're receiving valuable insight into becoming your best self!

Do you agree with the feedback you were given?

....

Was there anything in your feedback that surprised you?

....
....
....
....

If not, this is a good indicator that your self-reflective skills are insightful, and you should follow your instincts. If there was anything that surprised you, then use this as an opportunity to practise self-reflection more often.

Identify three items that you want to improve on from your self-reflection and feedback combined. Choose the ones that you think are most important, that will hold the most value for you moving forward and that align with your values. Write them down here in the order that you wish to address them from most important to least:

1. ....

2. ....

3. ....

Looking at your number 1 priority on the list above, what is your overall goal? Where do you want to be with this in three months' time, for example?

....

....

....

....

Working backwards from your three-month goal, identify what you want to have achieved in two months' time:

....

....

....

....

Working backwards from what you want to have achieved in two months' time, identify what you want to have achieved in one month's time:

....

....

....

....

> **TOP TIP**
>
> Remember! Your goals must be SMART. Refer to the chapter on goal setting for a reminder on SMART goal setting.

How will you know that you have been successful at each of your monthly goals? What are the indicators of success for you? Write them down here:

1 month: ....

2 months: ....

3 months: ....

Thinking about your overall goal, what opportunities do you have to practise this skill?

....

....

....

....

Thinking about your monthly goal and the opportunities you have identified to practise, what weekly/daily commitment will you make that will help you reach your monthly goal? (Set yourself a smaller goal that will help you reach the first month's indicator.)

....

....

....

....

....

....

Remember to make sure that this goal is SMART. If it is not achievable, you will quickly become disheartened, and this might throw you off your path to self-improvement. The smaller the goals, the more achievable they are. The quicker you see your hard work and progression, the more motivated you'll be to continue developing.

What barriers do you think you might be faced when you're working towards your first month's goal?

....

....

....

....

What solutions to overcoming these barriers can you think of that will help you feel prepared to work through them and continue your journey?

....

....

....

....

On a scale of 1 to 10, 1 being not at all confident, 10 being the most confident you've ever felt, how confident do you feel about achieving your first month's goal?

(1) (2) (3) (4) (5) (6) (7) (8) (9) (10)

Consider the number you have selected on the above scale. Is there anything that you think might help make you more confident in achieving your goal? What can you put in place that would help you move one more point up the scale and improve your confidence?

....

....

....

....

TOP TIP

Make sure you implement what you feel will help to improve your confidence in achieving your goal. You need to give yourself every opportunity for success.

Once you've implemented the strategies you identified as helpful to boost your confidence one more point up the scale, how confident do you now feel that you will achieve your goal?

(1) (2) (3) (4) (5) (6) (7) (8) (9) (10)

Review

Complete this section two weeks after starting work towards your goal (the half-way point to your one-month goal).

What are your reflections on the first two weeks of working towards your goal? What have you noticed about yourself?

....

....

....

....

....

....

Do you feel you are on track to meet your monthly goal?

....

If not, what can you put in place to help you with this?

....

....

....

....

It may be at this point that you're not on track because either the goal you have set yourself has changed or you may have underestimated the time it takes to develop and work towards this goal. That's okay; go back to your initial goal and make the changes required. This might mean extending the timeframe or changing your three-month, two-month and one-month goals to something smaller and moving your three-month goal to a six-month goal instead, for example.

What changes do you need to make?

....

....

....

....

When will you do this by?

....

Are there any resources you'll need to enable you to implement these changes and ensure you are back on track to achieve your goal?

....

....

....

....

If so, when will you obtain what you need to support you to move forward and implement the changes?

....

On a scale of 1 to 10, 1 being not at all confident, 10 being the most confident you could feel, how confident do you feel that you will meet your monthly target?

(1) (2) (3) (4) (5) (6) (7) (8) (9) (10)

What, if anything, can you implement to help you move up one more point on the scale, ensuring you feel more confident about achieving your goal?

....

....

....

....

When will you do this by?

....

Once you've implemented the strategies you identified as helpful to boost your confidence one more point up the scale, how confident do you now feel that you will achieve your goal?

(1) (2) (3) (4) (5) (6) (7) (8) (9) (10)

Are there any barriers you might come up against in the next two weeks that might prevent you reaching your desired target? Write them here:

....
....
....
....

What can you put in place that will ensure you can overcome these barriers and therefore remain on track to achieving your goal?

....
....
....
....

One-month review
Once you have reached the one-month point, complete the following section.

Did you achieve your goal?

....

What are your reflections? Were there any significant barriers? What did you learn?

....
....
....
....
....
....

How do you feel about your progress so far?

....
....
....
....

Is there anything you would do differently in the next month?

....

....

....

....

Do you feel you are on track to reach your two-monthly goal?

....

What can you do to ensure you reach your two-monthly goal?

....

....

....

....

Remember, if you're struggling at this point, review your original goals. If you feel they were not manageable for whatever reason, then scale them back to smaller, more achievable goals. We all have other commitments in our lives, whether that's looking after family members, caring for others, studying or working and much more. Achievable means what is achievable for *you*. It doesn't matter how long it takes you to get from A to B, all that matters is that you take the smallest steps in the right direction. This is a very personal journey and so the goals you set and the steps you take must be right for you.

On a scale of 1 to 10, 1 being not at all confident, 10 being as confident as you could be, how confident do you feel that you will reach your two-month goals?

① ② ③ ④ ⑤ ⑥ ⑦ ⑧ ⑨ ⑩

Is there anything you feel that you can do or put in place to help you feel more confidence for next month? If so, what will you commit to?

....

....

....

....

When will you do this by?

....

Does this conform to the SMART principles?

....

Can you put anything else in place to ensure this is the next *smallest* step towards your goal? Identify that here:

....

....

....

....

Now, how confident do you feel after implementing further strategies to support you in your second month?

① ② ③ ④ ⑤ ⑥ ⑦ ⑧ ⑨ ⑩

Thinking about your next month's goals, what is the first step you will take?

....

....

Identify the steps you will take to reach your two-month goals:

....

....

....

....

....

....

Remember to use time to split up your tasks into manageable chunks, for example week to week or day to day; make sure you work backwards from your goal to identify the steps you'll take.

How will you know that you have been successful in reaching your two-month goals? What indicators will you have of your success?

....

....

....

....

Do you anticipate any barriers to reaching your next set of goals? If so, what are they?

....

....

....

....

What plans can you put in place to overcome these barriers should they arise?

....

....

....

....

Having a strong plan in place to overcome barriers and preparing for the steps you're taking will help you in working towards this next set of goals – consistency is key and it is time to take those next steps now!

> **TOP TIP**
> Only ever concentrate on the next smallest step. Focusing too much on the bigger picture can lead you to becoming overwhelmed, and this can hinder your progress.

Two-month review

Once you have completed your second month of working towards your goal, complete the following section.

Did you meet your two-month goal?

....

How do you feel about your progress?

....

....

....

....

On reflection, is there anything that you would have done differently?

....

....

....

....

Thinking about what you would have done differently, what changes will you make moving into month three?

....

....

....

....

What opportunities do you have to implement these changes?

....

....

....

....

When will you do this by?

....

Have you noticed any significant developments in your relationships so far that are either positive or negative? Note them here:

....

....

....

....

Having worked towards your goals so far, have you identified anything from your interactions with others that you would like to focus more on or develop further?

....

....

....

....

On a scale of 1 to 10, 1 being not at all a priority, 10 being of the utmost importance, how much of a priority is this new development for you?

(1) (2) (3) (4) (5) (6) (7) (8) (9) (10)

Thinking about your overall goal for three months, will this new development help you achieve your overall goal?

....

Based on this, how important is this to you now? Does it need you to focus immediately on the new development or is it something that you would like to prioritise after the next four weeks?

....

....

What is your next step? Is it to continue on the path you set yourself or redirect towards this new skill/attribute?

....

....

Do you need to readjust your overall goal or extend the timeframe to ensure this is still achievable? If so, how?

....

....

....

....

Based on this, what do you need to do on a weekly/daily basis to reach your goal?

....

....

....

....

On a scale of 1 to 10, 1 being not at all committed, 10 being fully committed, how committed are you to meeting your next goal?

(1) (2) (3) (4) (5) (6) (7) (8) (9) (10)

What can you put in place that might help you move up to the next number on the scale (if it's not at its highest point so far)?

....

....

....

....

When will you do this by?

....

Is your goal/target SMART?

....

If not, how can you make this more achievable (the next *smallest* step)?

....

....

....

....

On a scale of 1 to 10, 1 being not at all confident, 10 being as confident as you could be, reflecting on the additional measures you have identified you'll put in place, how confident do you feel now? Has this moved up one point on your initial scale?

(1) (2) (3) (4) (5) (6) (7) (8) (9) (10)

What else can you do that will support you through this next month? Here you could consider reminders for yourself, prompts, visual cues in your day-to-day life to remind you of your goals or progress you have made or something to encourage you to continue on this journey. Write that down here:

....

....

....

....

When will you implement these by?

....

Implementing these strategies is crucial to your success because you are now giving yourself every opportunity to reach or even exceed your goals.

TOP TIP
Give yourself permission to support yourself and be your own biggest fan!

Three-month review
The time has come to review your overall progress. Fill in this section after you've completed your three-month challenge.

What positive changes have you found in your relationships so far?

....

....

....

....

On a scale of 1 to 10, 1 being no progress made at all, 10 being the best you could have done, how do you rate your progress?

(1) (2) (3) (4) (5) (6) (7) (8) (9) (10)

Are you surprised by the outcomes of your goal or the progress you have made? If so, explain why here:

....
....
....
....

Did you miss out any of the steps that you planned for these three months?

....

If so, why?

....
....
....
....

Did this help or hinder your progress? Explain why here:

....
....
....
....

Reflecting on this, what will you change moving forward?

....
....
....
....

What have you learnt about yourself over the past three months?

....
....
....
....

What are you proud of?

....

....

....

....

Do you see a different future for yourself in relation to your relationships with others?

....

....

....

....

What impact do you think this will have on your future?

....

....

....

....

What commitments do you want to make to yourself for the future? Write them here:

....

....

....

....

....

....

How will you ensure that you remain consistent with your commitments?

....

....

....

....

....

....

Is this a SMART goal for you?

....

Identify anything that you think will ensure your commitments are SMART:

....

....

....

....

Thinking about all that you have learnt and your reflections so far, identify goals for the next three months that will help you build, maintain, repair or enhance any of the relationships in your life, including any new relationships you'd like to build:

....

....

....

....

....

....

Using the principles that you have learnt in this chapter, work through the same process to work towards your preferred future. You can use these methods repeatedly, building upon your progress every three months to reach new heights in your relationships. Learning and developing skills and attributes and building or starting new relationships are things that you don't reach an end point with. Relationships require some maintenance even if it's the smallest amount: for example, the one phone call a year to the person in your life who you can pick up where you left off with after what seems like a lifetime – that phone call is still maintenance within a relationship. Relationships can enhance our lives and bring a world full of opportunity, special moments and a sense of satisfaction and purpose. So, use what you've learnt here to get the most out of yours.

Understanding relationships

Whilst building, maintaining or repairing relationships are important, it's also important to distinguish between relationships that should and need to be repaired and those that cause significant harm: that are toxic and destructive for your mental health and wellbeing. It can be incredibly difficult to cut ties with some people, especially if they play an integral part in your life or you rely on them for essential support. It can also be a challenge to spot the signs of toxic relationships in any context.

Some of the traits you may see or experience in toxic relationships can be:

+ Lack of support.
+ Toxic communication such as being disrespectful, sarcastic or overcritical.
+ Jealousy.
+ Resentment.
+ Dishonesty.
+ Making big financial decisions without discussion.
+ Ignoring what you need.
+ Feeling like you are walking on eggshells.

Dealing with issues like these within relationships is damaging to your self-esteem, confidence and overall wellbeing. It can be challenging to recognise signs of toxic relationships, particularly if you're exposed to these traits in more than one individual. Being around people who are unwilling to support your personal development will hold you back from achieving your goals. It uses a lot of emotional energy to distance yourself from others who show these behavioural traits, but if you want more from your life and want to achieve your goals, it is essential to start to move away from people who don't support your development and long-term aspirations. Relationships with anyone, whether that's a partner or friend, should be uplifting, supportive and kind.

If you've identified that for you to develop as a person you need to end some relationships, that is also okay and a positive thing. You don't have to be the person who is compromising your values, self-esteem, confidence or resources to please others if you don't get anything positive in return. Relationships are about balance or civility, at least in relationships such as work ones where you might not want to go out socially with that person but you still need to work together for a common goal.

One way of identifying whether relationships are working for you as well as for the other person is to consider a personal contract. This identifies what values are important to you and what your expectations are within relationships, and helps you to remain accountable to yourself, holding yourself to the standards that you set.[1]

Personal contract

Identify what is important to you in your relationships. Think about behaviours that you would like to receive from other people. Think about the basic requirements that you expect from others when starting, building and maintaining relationships and write them down here:

....

....

....

....

....

....

Write down three commitments to yourself when entering or whilst in relationships that will empower you in holding yourself accountable for the ways you are treated. Use 'I' statements here, for example, 'I am worthy of respect':

....

....

....

....

....

....

Thinking about these three standards, how are you going to ensure that you are treated with the basic requirements that you expect from others in relationships? For example, if you don't get what you need in terms of basic respect, what will you do?

....

....

....

....

---

1   If you're worried about any of your relationships and need support, contact your local advice centre for support to access services that may be able to help.

....

....

Communication and personal boundaries are crucial in relationships where you're not happy or feel you need something more or different. You can still use the steps in this chapter to work on ending or repairing relationships if you use the principles of the method. Use a small steps approach, gain support from others in your life, concentrate on the next smallest step (it doesn't matter how small) and execute your plan. Use the resources of your social group, community or even professional support agencies to help you plan, ensuring this is SMART.

SNAPSHOT

- 📷 Living authentically means to be true to yourself, whatever that looks like!
- 📷 Reflecting on the relationships in your life will help you to cut out people who don't share your vision for yourself and your personal development and fill it with people who do!
- 📷 Relationships can be complex and challenging at times, but they can also bring joy to you and enhance your life in ways you might not have even imagined yet!
- 📷 Relationships need maintenance, and repairing the ones that are important to you will strengthen them in the future.
- 📷 Sometimes you must have relationships with others that you might not necessarily choose to associate with. However, remember to see the bigger goal, especially if these are work-related relationships and the key to your success at work is reliant upon others in the team.

• Chapter 7 •

Finances

Financial stability is essential for reducing stress and reaching your financial goals. Financial goals might seem like a strange concept living in the modern world surrounded by consumerism, pay-day loans and credit agreements available for you to buy whatever you want, whenever you want. Financial instability is a big cause of stress for many people, from being in debt to not having enough money to pay the bills or for general day-to-day living costs. Having financial goals can help bring some financial stability to your life, relieve the stress of everyday money worries and help you reach a point where you are comfortable – whatever that looks like for you. Success isn't about what material goods someone has, whether they've got a fancy car or a big house; if you're riddled with debt and stress as a result of having those things, how can you enjoy what you've worked for if you owe money to multiple lenders? Success is whatever you perceive success to be, not what society says it is. For you that might be the fancy car and the big house; for others it might be living debt free – it's an individual and personal concept.

What does financial success look like for you?

....

....

....

....

....

....

If you're struggling with this question, visualise your preferred future: do you want to be debt free, make a big purchase like a car or a house, invest in a business or even live in a smaller property or alternative accommodation so you can reduce the number of hours you work and enjoy the time you have?

Thinking about your bigger financial goals is what will help you work backwards to determine smaller steps to your preferred future.

To obtain your preferred future in respect of your finances, what resources do you need?

....

....

....

....

Is there anyone that can help you obtain the resources you need? List them here:

....

....

....

....

Remember, you can ask someone that you trust or someone that has an interest in financial affairs for advice on how you might obtain the resources you need. Knowledge is power!

From your list of resources that will help you obtain your preferred future, write down what you need to prioritise first:

....

....

Do you need any additional resources to obtain this first step?

....

....

What options do you have for obtaining these?

....

....

....

....

Think about savings, additional income, advice and guidance, qualifications, practical resources and so on. Working backwards from this, what steps do you need to take to obtain the resources you need to start working on your preferred future?

....

....

....

....

....

....

Therefore, what will your first financial goal be? Don't forget to make it SMART:

....

....

....

....

Understanding the wider goal (your preferred future) and breaking it down into two to three stages of obtaining resources to reach your first goal and overall outcome helps you to reframe your thinking and take more manageable steps towards your preferred future.

> **TOP TIP**
>
> It doesn't matter if obtaining this part takes you a long time to achieve; what matters is that you are consistently taking small steps to obtain what you need for you to then take your next step.

Budgeting skills

Budgeting is a key life skill. Some people are naturally good at budgeting. At the other end of the scale, others live beyond their means; this can cause significant financial stress, which in turn can have a detrimental impact on your wellbeing. Ignoring financial worries and carrying on with the same destructive habits that may have caused the stress in the first place will only make matters worse and prolong the struggle.

Budgeting skills may seem like a very basic topic to cover; however, according to Financial Capability UK, 39 per cent of adults in the UK don't feel confident managing their money, with nearly 9 million people in serious debt.[1] So, like the other strategies in this book, starting with the basics with a preferred future in mind is an excellent strategy to use to begin to address issues.

Financial stability or working towards your preferred future is relevant here, because if you want to achieve your life and personal goals, you'll need to be able to manage your finances effectively, especially if your goals are to invest in a business, or work self-employed on a project that you're passionate about, or if you just want less stress in your day-to-day life.

Start to understand your finances by completing a monthly income vs expenditure analysis. In the income section, write down all sources of money, whether that's from working, benefits or any other source. In the expenditure section, write down any expenses that you pay out for. Think about food, bills, finance agreements, loans, money owed to friends/family/others as well as any subscriptions, gym memberships, TV packages, and so on.

Income

Date	Income source	Amount

Expenditure

Date	Expense	Amount

1   www.fincap.org.uk/en/articles/key-statistics-on-uk-financial-capability

What is your total income?

....

What is your total expenditure?

....

How do these compare? Do you have more income than expenses or more expenses than income?

....

Looking at your finances now, how does it make you feel?

....

....

....

....

Is there anything new that you've now thought of from doing this exercise that you would like to work towards as part of your preferred financial future? Use visualisation to help you in this section:

....

....

....

....

....

....

If so, complete the steps to finalising your goal. Make your goal SMART:

....

....

....

....

....

....

Review the goal: does it cover everything that the SMART acronym suggests? Is it specific, measurable, achievable, realistic and timely? Could you make it more SMART?

....

....

....

....

Split your goal into smaller timeframes. What does this look like? Monthly? Weekly? Daily?

....

....

....

....

....

What do you need to do every day to achieve your first financial goal in relation to income and expenditure?

....

....

....

....

In one month's time, what will you have achieved?

....

....

In two months' time, what will you have achieved?

....

....

In three months' time, what will you have achieved?

....

....

Does your goal need to change at this point to ensure you meet your longer-term goal?

....

If so, what does your next three-month goal look like now?

....

....

....

....

What does your six-month goal look like now?

....

....

....

....

Based on your new goals, what will you have achieved after one year from the point when you made your first goal?

....

....

....

....

Based on this, what does your first small step look like?

....

....

....

....

Do you need any resources, or do you need to speak to anyone to help support you to achieve this goal? If so, what do you need and who do you need to speak to?

....

....

....

When will you do this by?

....

Now you've got your first goals to your preferred future that will help you make changes over the year. Remember, consistency and commitment are what will help you achieve your preferred future; it won't happen overnight. If your circumstances change and you need to review your goals, then you can use the above exercise to do this. It doesn't matter how long it takes you to get to your preferred future. One small step each day is a step towards what you want to achieve.

Savings

Using the income vs expenditure sheet to calculate every penny of income and expenditure is one way in which you can help highlight what you're spending your money on. It can help you decide whether you need to cut back on a few things to help you save more, invest in something for your future, buy something you want for the future such as somewhere to live or a car, or even just help you save a nest egg for rainy days.

You can budget your income by using different 'pots' to split it up into over the course of the month. This can be useful if you're saving up for a holiday, want to ensure that you're not overspending on clothes/takeaways/coffee or if you want to save up for something bigger like a house. Some online banks offer a 'pots' feature as part of their packages, but this can be done without changing your bank and with a commitment to self-control. Reframing your income in this way can help give a different perspective on your finances, and as we've learnt in other chapters, reframing is an essential tool to help you gain insight into what you want your preferred future to look like, as well as to give meaning to what you're trying to achieve.

Having understood what you are spending your money on, is there anything that you want to cut back on that would help you reach your preferred financial future?

....

....

....

....

What SMART goal could you set around this? For example, if you get a takeaway once a week, can you get a takeaway once a month instead? The money you save can be put into a pot of your choosing to help you work towards your preferred future:

....

....

....

....

....

....

What do you want for your preferred future? More cash to spend generally? A dream holiday? A house? A car? Investment in stocks/shares or even your own business?

....

....

....

....

....

....

TOP TIP

Your goals for the future don't have to be based on something materialistic. You might want more financial stability, which comes with less worry about money each month – what matters is that it is *your* financial future, not anyone else's, so make sure it reflects what you want.

Knowing what you spend your money on is the first step to understanding how you can manage your finances better. With your above goals in mind, choose what pots you want to have that link with your preferred future goals. Based on your future goals, what pots would work best for you? Here are some ideas:

Bills/day-to-day costs	Eating out	Wedding	Savings
Clothes	Investments (any)	Start a business	Transport
Entertainment	Holidays	Buy a home	Surgery

....
....
....
....

Are there any categories that are not listed that you want to use for one of your pots? List them here:

....
....

Write down the pots you want to use here, choosing a maximum of five if you're doing this exercise for the first time. When you get used to separating your money and achieving your first year's goals, you can increase the pots to help you reach your next goals. One of your pots should be your day-to-day spending and bills, because this will be a significant part of your income needed to live and therefore has to be considered in any financial exercise:

1. ....
2. ....
3. ....
4. ....
5. ....

Identify first what percentage of your income needs to be spent on bills/transport/ food/utilities. What is that percentage? ....

What percentage of your income is left over? ....

Understanding the money you have that can be classed as disposable (the amount you have left over when essential payments have been made) will help you to understand what money you can set aside into each of your pots.

Split up your disposable income percentage into smaller percentages – what percentage of your income do you want to go into your other pots? Write this next to your pots in the list above. The percentages don't have to be equal; split them based on what's most important to you and what you want to work on first, for example saving for a wedding or holiday of a lifetime, or even just having some savings.

Once you've understood what percentage of your income you want to go into each of your pots it's time to understand the value of your percentages.

Going back to your list of pots, calculate how much money you will put into each of the pots every month. If you've got any money left over or if you've gone over budget for this exercise, revisit the income vs expenditure section and ensure you account for every penny of income and expenditure you have each month. Think about your longer-term goals. Calculate how much money you will have in each of your pots after three months:

1. ....
2. ....
3. ....
4. ....
5. ....

Now do the same for six months:

1. ....
2. ....
3. ....
4. ....
5. ....

And, after one year, how much money will you have in those pots?

1. ....
2. ....
3. ....
4. ....
5. ....

Based on this scoping exercise, will you have reached your financial goal for the year? If not, revisit your initial goal and work through the exercises again, making some amendments. You might not have managed to save for your house in one year, but as in all the other exercises, think about the bigger picture and work backwards to achieve your goals. What are your five-year financial goals?

....

....

....

....

What are your ten-year financial goals?

....

....

....

....

Working backwards from these, does your first year's goal fit into your five- and ten-year goals? If not, what do you need to change in your first year that will set you on a trajectory to achieving your longer-term plans?

....

....

....

....

Use the one- to three-year goal-setting strategies above to plan out each year up to your five- to ten-year financial strategy to understand if you will meet your longer-term goal. Planning and tracking are essential to managing your finances. If you don't have a plan, you'll spend your money in ways that might bring you short-term fulfilment but not necessarily help you with your longer-term goals.

Review

Once you've completed your first year (and subsequent ones moving towards your longer-term goals) it's important to conduct a review. Use these questions to conduct one-month, three-month and six-month reviews also.

Did you meet your first year's goals?

....

What happened?

....

....

....

How do you feel now?

....
....
....
....

What did you learn on your journey?

....
....
....
....
....
....

What will you change moving forward in your next year?

....
....
....
....

Have your longer-term goals now changed because you've moved towards your preferred future in year 1?

....
....

What do these goals now look like?

....
....
....
....

Will this affect your longer-term five- to ten-year strategy?

....
....

....

....

What will your set of goals for the next year look like?

....

....

....

....

Remember! Make sure they're SMART!

Saving is a part of the financial world that is often talked about, but many people struggle to save for many different reasons. A lot of factors of modern life impact on people's ability to save money, from increased living costs to debt and everything in between. Understanding where your finances are in the exercises you've done above will help you determine if you can save any money and if you want to!

As in other areas of this book, reframing and using different techniques can help you approach your goals differently, and the same is applicable to savings. If you've got a savings goal as part of your preferred financial future planning and have completed how much you can save each month (realistically and without dipping into it every month), then you've set yourself a solid foundation. Others find it easier to use strategies such as Martin Lewis's (money expert) Christmas Saving tips. Martin Lewis has devised a 1p challenge whereby you start by saving 1p on 1 January, then 2p on 2 January, 3p on 3 January and so on throughout the year, increasing it by 1p every day. You put this in a separate pot and by the end of December you'll have £667.95.[2] Challenging yourself can help with motivation to save and makes it a little bit more fun! You can even adapt challenges like the 1p challenge to suit your financial situation. You could do it backwards, for example, starting on the first day by saving £3.65. Refraining from your daily coffee on your commute and choosing to make a drink at home or work instead can help you to set aside this money so you've got a bit extra by the end of the year.

Debt

Debt can be incredibly debilitating, but it can also help you towards your preferred future if it is used wisely. For example, if you get a credit card to buy all the things you've ever dreamed of, but you know that your income doesn't match what you

---

2   www.moneysavingexpert.com/team-blog/2019/12/the-1p-365-day-savings-challenge

can pay off every month and you're paying high interest rates, this won't serve you well. However, if you get a credit card to improve your credit rating and display self-control around your spending, only using it to cover expenses that you already have the cash to pay off the card with in full each month, this will improve your credit rating over time. This can help you gain credit in the future that might help you with a big purchase such as if you choose to buy a house, for example. Debt such as student loans can be seen as an investment in your future.

Obtaining some debt isn't always a bad thing, but you should ensure that any financial decisions around getting into debt are taken seriously and that you've weighed up all the consequences, both positive and negative, before deciding. You should consider the following when thinking about taking on the debt:

- ✦ Will it help you reach your future goals (such as a student loan to pay for education)?
- ✦ Will it have a detrimental impact on your day-to-day living? For example, if you won't be able to afford to feed yourself every day then this would have a detrimental impact. Remember, health is wealth!
- ✦ Consider whether the debt is manageable and you can afford to pay it off each month.
- ✦ Is the interest rate too high? If you're not able to afford a loan because of the high interest rate, scale back your goal to improving your credit rating in the first year, for example. This will then help you obtain better loan rates in the future, which will be more manageable financially and help you achieve your preferred future without significant impact on your finances.

Understanding your debt and becoming free from debt that has an impact on your financial stability is essential to reaching your preferred future. Organisations like Citizens Advice Bureau (CAB) can help you understand your debt and are also able to advise you on debt consolidation. If you're in a significant amount of debt that is causing stress and affecting your life, you can discuss with CAB how you can become debt free or get to a point where your debt is manageable by consolidating it. This comes with financial consequences so always discuss this with an impartial advisor first!

Your financial goals need to be personal to you. It doesn't matter whether it's to consolidate your debt and pay it off over a long period of time so you can work on another financial goal or if you're saving for a big event: they must be personal to you and benefit you to ensure you have the motivation to achieve them. If they're not personal to you and bring you no benefit, it is more likely that you'll struggle to reach your goals.

Your bigger vision for financial freedom can be a source of motivation for those days that you find challenging – think about the bigger picture and scale it back to what you would do every single day to get there. Consistency and small steps are the key!

Side hustle

More and more people are starting to set up their own small businesses as 'side hustles' to their main source of income and are doing it for lots of reasons: either to increase their income generally or because they enjoy what they're doing and have decided to turn a profit as a bonus.

Many people are starting to see that their business idea, no matter how small, can come to fruition with some basic business planning, a basic understanding of finances, and the will and desire to make it work!

Do you have something that you're passionate about that you could sell as a side hustle? Think about things you're good at and that you enjoy spending time on, or if you've got a particular set of skills that you can sell as a consultant or trainer. Write your ideas down here:

....

....

....

....

....

....

Does the prospect of starting your own side hustle excite you?

....

What are the benefits for you of having a side hustle?

....

....

....

....

....

....

What are the downsides to starting a side hustle?

....

....

....

....

....

....

If things like finances to buy equipment/materials/resources are holding you back from starting your business, then use that as an opportunity to set yourself some goals to accumulate what you need before you start your side hustle. These could include the financial goals above and you could include setting aside a pot that you invest in (no matter how small the investment is) that will then help you get what you need to start.

Where could you sell your product/service?

....

....

....

....

What opportunities, resources or support do you need from others?

....

....

....

....

....

....

Starting a side hustle can be time consuming, so it's important that you've chosen something you're passionate about as this will help give you the motivation and strength to move forward with your goals. Having a side hustle based on something you enjoy can turn a hobby into a profit!

If you've got an idea, then commit it to paper. The best way to help you understand if your side hustle is a realistic possibility is to write a simple business plan.

Business plan templates are available online as free downloads, and there are many other resources on platforms such as Google and YouTube that can help you to research business strategy and understand how others have created their side hustles too.

If you're not sure about how you could start a side hustle but want to, do some research online about what others have done. You could also think about your experiences as a gender diverse person; there are many things that transgender people need that help to make their lives easier on a day-to-day basis. Maybe you could write a book, or you might have an idea for an invention that would help with gender affirmation, for example. Think about your experiences and what you would have found useful throughout transitioning and whether there is anything you could consider bringing to market to help others.

Side hustles are a great way to test out what it would be like to run a business but on a smaller scale. So, if you are planning on having your own business in the future, scale it down to a smaller-scale project, as you've done with your other goals, working backwards from the bigger picture to a smaller project and using it as a testing phase. Starting a side hustle will bring you lots of experience; you'll learn a lot around what it takes to run a business and you'll also learn a lot about yourself! Use this as an opportunity to learn about what you'll need for the future, what it takes to run your own business and how you might use the lessons you learn from your side hustle to inform your business plan when you're ready to take those next steps.

SNAPSHOT

- Setting yourself financial goals that are clear, concise and SMART can help you towards your preferred future.
- Understanding your income vs expenditure is a great starting point to understanding your financial capability and organising your finances.
- Challenging yourself helps to bring motivation and a bit of fun to your journey.
- There's good debt and bad debt. You can help yourself get out of bad debt to then work towards your preferred future – getting some independent advice can help you sort out your finances.
- Investments in yourself can help you reach financial freedom and stability, such as student loans to learn a new trade/profession.
- Having a side hustle can turn a passion or a hobby into a money-making venture.
- Use a side hustle as a test run if you're planning to develop a business in the future – the lessons learnt from having a side hustle can help you envisage future challenges and therefore help you plan to overcome them.

• Chapter 8 •

Career Goals and Aspirations

Career development

Building a career for yourself can be challenging and exciting. Working towards career development and finding or developing what you are passionate about can be incredibly fulfilling and help you realise what you're capable of when you set your goals and reach them. Working towards your career goals can also help you learn more about yourself as a person, what you enjoy doing, or what to steer away from as you work through the steps towards your preferred future. The process can be incredibly rewarding, and as you move through the steps, you'll see that you're capable of more than you initially gave yourself credit for and may find something you're passionate about.

Every step you take helps you achieve a new level of success and growth as a person. Transitioning alone can help you understand that you have the resilience, emotional intelligence and strength to take control of your life and achieve whatever you set your mind to.

The world of work and employment can be a hostile place for gender diverse people, and the facts are that, as in other areas of life, transgender people are discriminated against within the employment sector, whether that's when gaining employment or within the workplace. This can be a barrier to people gaining and progressing in employment because fear, often rooted in other people's horror stories, can hold them back. While we must be realistic and understand that life can be hostile for the gender diverse community, one of the most important skills to learn and develop is to live in your world and no one else's; don't let other people's fears prevent your progress. It is important to face any challenges one step at a time.

In this section, we'll look at devising your career development plan as well as skill building. This could be around whether you want your dream job, a promotion or to start your own business. Anything is possible here so think big, and as you've done in the other sections of this book, work backwards from your goal to understand the steps you need to take to achieve each of your smaller goals leading to the destination.

To build your career development plan, it's important first to understand where you are now, what skills you have and what you need to work on to achieve your career goals.

What is your current role? Are you in employment or training, or currently unemployed?

....

....

If you could click your fingers and your career dreams had come true overnight, what would this look like for you?

....

....

....

....

....

....

If you're unsure of your answer for this, you can leave it blank and work through the rest of the section first to see if you can identify what you are good at and what your passion is and then answer the question. You can also take the UCAS Careers Quiz to find out what personality traits and skills you have that would give you some ideas about what roles you might be interested in.[1]

Continuing with the 'where are you now?' theme, what is currently holding you back (if anything) from achieving your career goals?

....

....

....

---

1   www.ucas.com/careers/careers-quiz

....

....

....

Think about this barrier in a practical way and categorise it. Does it fall into any of the following categories?

Financial	Self-esteem	Confidence	Lack of time
Education	Skills	Qualifications	

....

....

....

....

It could be that you don't feel confident enough to follow your dreams or you are struggling with your self-esteem, in which case, go back to the chapter on self-esteem and confidence and re-do it with your career goals in mind. It could be that you don't yet have the necessary skills, qualifications or experience required to achieve your career goal or that you don't have the financial means to start your own business or gain your qualification. If any of your barriers to achieving the next steps are rooted in any of the chapters that we've covered already in the book, go back to those and re-do the activities with your career goals in mind. This will help you to overcome these challenges before continuing with this chapter.

Looking back at your career plan goals, what do you need by way of resources to achieve your dream job/start your own business? Think about skills, qualifications, courses you might need to take, or if you're looking at a promotion within your current role, what is it specifically that needs to happen for you to get there?

....

....

....

....

....

....

Working through this book, and especially in this chapter, you'll see that the emphasis is on your responsibility to understand what you can do to reach your goals. If you feel that it is your boss that's holding you back or that someone doesn't like you and that's why you can't get your promotion, then work through the self-esteem and confidence chapter again with this in mind. You have skills that employers will pay for; maybe it's time to move companies and work for one that will invest in you and your development. If this is the case, use this as a focus for working through this chapter, identifying your next steps in gaining a new job.

As we've done throughout the book, let's work backwards from your bigger goals to identify the smaller steps required to get there. Remember, make it SMART!

On a scale of 1–10, 1 being not at all confident, 10 being as confident as you could be, how confident do you feel to move forward with achieving your career goals at this point?

(1) (2) (3) (4) (5) (6) (7) (8) (9) (10)

Thinking about your overall goal, what do you think are the steps you need to take to get there? Again, think about any qualifications or experience you might need, any financial resources you need, any support from others and research you might need to do. You might even need to have a conversation with a key person in your life. Identify the steps here:

1. ....
2. ....
3. ....
4. ....
5. ....
6. ....

Thinking about your first step, what resources do you need to make this happen? Think critically and identify every resource that needs to be at your disposal so you can move forward:

....
....
....

....
....
....

It's crucial that the resources you need are prioritised. You won't need everything all at once, you only need enough resources to take the first step. So, looking at your list, put them in order of what is most important now:

....
....
....
....
....
....

Let's break this down further into how you'll get what you need to take that first step. If it's additional finances, then some research around financial planning/options might be useful (student loan research, for example, if you're looking for a qualification). Or if it is a practical resource that you require, what is available in the local community to help you? Do you need to conduct some research that will help you gain the necessary resources? Write down what you need to do first here that will help you overcome the barrier you're facing in taking your first step:

....
....
....
....

Thinking back to the SMART acronym, how can you make the step towards obtaining the resources you need SMART? Write down your SMART action here:

....
....
....
....

Your initial plan identified the first step you felt you needed to take towards your goal; however, looking at the resources you need and understanding the barriers you are facing, what is the first step now on reflection?

....

....

Do you foresee any barriers or issues that will stop you from achieving this first step?

....

....

....

....

....

....

If so, what are possible solutions to these potential barriers?

....

....

....

....

....

....

Understanding potential issues along the way and having a contingency plan if they should happen will help you feel less overwhelmed and more focused. Knowing what you can do to overcome bumps in the road and help you remain on the path you've set yourself will help you achieve your goals. It is unusual to be able to go from A to B without any issues along the way, so planning for these can help you feel more in control of the future and leaves you feeling more confident that you can overcome them.

When will you achieve your first step by?

....

On a scale of 1–10, 1 being not at all confident, 10 being as confident as you could be, how confident do you feel now that you've made a plan of action to move forward?

(1) (2) (3) (4) (5) (6) (7) (8) (9) (10)

Has this improved from the first career goals scale that you just did? If not, what needs to happen or what do you need for you to enable you to feel more confident that you can do this, and to move up to the next number on your scale?

....

....

....

....

If you're struggling here, go back through your plan and review whether your steps are SMART. Remember, the steps are supposed to be small: the smaller, the better so that they are achievable and realistic.

Once you have achieved the first step of your step-by-step plan as identified in the goals exercise, look at your second step on the list and work through the activities again, identifying resources and potential problems and scaling your steps down to smaller, manageable steps.

Review the steps

After you've completed each of the steps in your original plan, it's important that you take time to reflect on and review your progress. Reflecting on your progress helps to identify what you have learnt and therefore what you can change as you progress with your other steps. This also helps to improve self-esteem and confidence, because as you work through your steps you'll start to see results of your hard work, and this will give you the confidence to understand that you are a powerful resource in your own life.

On a scale of 1–10, 1 being not at all challenging, 10 being extremely challenging, how challenging did you find completing your first step?

(1) (2) (3) (4) (5) (6) (7) (8) (9) (10)

Is there anything that would have made the process easier?

....

....

....

What skills have you developed by moving through the process of achieving the steps in your plan?

....
....
....
....

What have you learnt about yourself that will help you with your next step?

....
....
....
....

What, if anything, will you change to make the process of progressing through your next steps easier?

....
....
....
....

On a scale of 1 to 10, 1 being not at all confident, 10 being as confident as you could be, how confident do you feel in taking your next step now?

(1) (2) (3) (4) (5) (6) (7) (8) (9) (10)

If you don't feel that you can scale yourself at a 10, what one thing can you do or put in place that will help you scale yourself at one point higher?

....
....
....
....

As before, as you move through your step-by-step plan, make sure that you complete the review after each of the steps. That way, when you progress with your personal and career development plans, you can reflect, learn and change things to make the process easier for the next stage.

Skill building

Building your skills over time becomes an important asset for businesses, organisations and your personal development. This will also support you if you want to start your own business or you're looking for that promotion.

Companies are looking for people who can use their own initiative, and they want to invest in the development of people who want to invest in themselves. So what you do outside of work and within work to build on your skills is vital.

Joel Trammell, founder and CEO of Khorus Software, states that whilst every job has its own specific set of skill requirements, managers look for the following six key attributes in all employees, regardless of their position:[2]

1. Being able to deliver results: doing what you say you're going to do, and if you can't meet a deadline, communicating this as early as possible to line managers.
2. Being a good team player: supporting others, playing your part within the team and not causing issues or conflicts within teams.
3. Being able to use your own initiative: this frees up the manager's time and makes way for new ideas, which brings opportunities for growth to the company.
4. Honesty and integrity: doing what you say you're going to do, and speaking up if there are issues so they can be addressed quickly and prevented from getting worse so that any damage to the business is limited.
5. Enthusiasm: employers value employees who are positive and passionate about the roles they play within the organisation.
6. Dedication: this means employees who treat their job as part of their career, are committed to improving their skills and increasing their value, and who serve as a role model for others in the company.

As people progress into management and leadership roles an additional set of values and skills is required, but the six qualities above are a strong foundation to build upon.

---

2   www.inc.com/joel-trammell/6-things-every-manager-wants-from-employees.html

Taking responsibility

Taking responsibility is a key skill that you'll need in any part of your life, but it will especially help you within the workplace. We hear the phrase 'taking responsibility' quite often but to truly understand its meaning and put this into practice can be difficult. It takes a lot of self-reflection to understand what you should take responsibility for and what you can do to role model that responsibility to others.

Taking responsibility means understanding what part you play in your team and what you personally acknowledge as your successes but also your failures. For example, if you've not met a deadline either at or outside of work, being able to reflect on why you didn't meet that deadline without blaming others, and reflecting on what you could have done differently, is accepting responsibility for your project. Sometimes if someone hasn't done something that you needed for your work project this does have an impact on you; but you still need to take responsibility for the fact that you might not have delivered on what you said you were going to do.

The term 'taking responsibility' is often seen in a negative light, but if we reframe this, it also means accepting responsibility for your successes as well. The hard work you have put into a project or your own development is worth something, and being able to accept that wholeheartedly can sometimes be more challenging than you think. Acknowledging your own success helps to build self-esteem, confidence and an understanding that when you put effort into something and dedicate yourself to your goals, you can accomplish and overcome things you never thought were possible.

Reflect on a recent project or goal that you said you were going to achieve. What happened?

....
....
....
....
....
....

What were the barriers that stopped you from achieving your goal?

....
....

....

....

Was reaching your goal reliant on someone else supporting that?

....

What did they do or not do that affected your performance?

....

....

....

....

How could you have supported that person to deliver on their responsibilities?

....

....

....

....

Could you have done anything differently that would have meant you met that goal? What was your part in this?

....

....

....

....

How can you ensure that you deliver next time?

....

....

....

....

Time management

Time management is an important skill if you're going to manage multiple goals and reach your overall potential. Being able to manage your time – being on time for meetings or for work, or meeting important deadlines – shows a level of organ-isational skills as well as proving to those around you that you are serious about meeting your goals. Managing your time well also shows your employer that you are reliable and are taking your responsibilities to yourself and the organisation you work for seriously. It projects the image that you are committed to helping the business reach their goals too. Being able to show your employer that you are reliable, dedicated and committed to their projects will support your career development.

Time management is linked with organisational skills: the more organised you are, the better you'll be able to manage your time. If you're the type of person that leaves everything to the last minute and runs around frantically trying to pull together your final presentation, or you didn't prepare the night before to get to a new destination on time, then developing your organisational skills is crucial for your success.

Let's reflect on where you are currently. Has there been a recent experience where you feel you should have prepared yourself better, and if you had, a better outcome of the situation would have been more likely? Write down the scenario here:

....

....

....

....

....

....

What went wrong?

....

....

....

....

....

....

What went well?

....

....

....
....
....
....

Everyone has their own way to organise and manage their time, and there are many different strategies that you can learn, and test, to perfect your own strategy. It's important that you try different strategies to find what works best for you. Here are some tips to get you started:

- Write down what you need to achieve each week. Break this down into smaller goals. For example, if you need to be somewhere on time the following day, think about what you can do the night before that will help you best prepare for the morning. This could be making sure you go to sleep early, ensuring your bags are packed with everything you need for the day and making your lunch if necessary. Once your day is over, reflect on how you felt having prepared for the tasks ahead. What went well? What could have been improved? How did you feel being more prepared?
- Get into a routine. Effective time management is rooted in having a positive routine. Work performance is affected by what you do in your personal time. If you're not getting enough sleep and waking up with minutes to spare before you need to leave for work, then you're likely to be stressed and tired, end up missing breakfast, spending too much money buying lunch every day, and therefore being tired and not eating well, which affects daily performance. Everything you do or don't do has a consequence that can either improve your performance or hold you back. The performance chapter of this book will help you build a strong routine for reaching your goals.
- Go to bed earlier and make sure you're getting enough quality sleep – ban technology in your bedroom and create a healthy sleeping environment to promote sleep.
- Prepare everything the night before – especially if the following day is particularly crucial to reaching your goals.

Being able to prioritise your work/life tasks can help you to become more productive. Highlighting deadlines in your diary and breaking down the work into smaller chunks over time helps larger tasks become more manageable. Also, resisting the temptation to do the tasks you enjoy doing first as opposed to the ones that are more important and have a shorter deadline can help you make sure you're not frantically working until late at night to complete the tasks you didn't want to do.

One of the ways in which you can support yourself to prioritise your tasks and deadlines is to utilise the Eisenhower Matrix. This categorises tasks according to whether they are: Urgent or Not Urgent, and Important or Not Important. By categorising your tasks, you can effectively prioritise your tasks to meet your deadlines. Here is an example of how the matrix works:

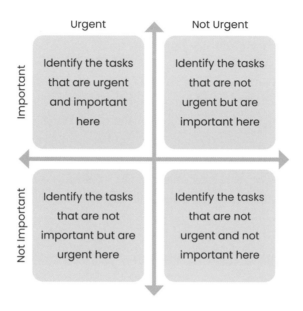

To use the matrix, you need to place each of the tasks into the box that corresponds with the most appropriate label.

Once you've identified the status of each task, you can write your to do list and work through the tasks one by one, starting with the urgent and important tasks first.

People are generally very busy at work so taking some time out to do an activity like this can feel counterproductive and that you could use the time more effectively by completing a task you need to do. However, exercises like this do not take long at all, and the more organised you are with your tasks and prioritising them, the more time it will save you in the long term. Not prioritising them leads to a chaotic and stressful work and home life. The more time you invest in organising yourself, your work and home life, the more effectively you'll use your time; so you'll feel less stressed, achieve more and have time left over to do the things you want to do!

> **TOP TIP**
> The more time you invest in organising your time, the more you will achieve.

Teamwork

Teamwork is a requirement of most jobs. The ability to work as a team player and take on different roles within a team to achieve a task is crucial to the success of any organisation so you'll often see this cited as a requirement in person specifications. It takes a team to achieve many things in life as well as work, whether that's someone giving you moral support or providing you with resources, advice and information to help you on your journey. So having the ability to work with people and play your part within a team is essential.

For any team to be effective, different people need to play different roles within it. If you have a team of leaders, everyone will be fighting to lead the team rather than focusing on completing the goals; equally if you have a team of workers without a leader, there will be no focus or plan to get to the end goal.

Meredith Belbin identifies nine key roles that make teams effective:[3]

1. Plant: creates ideas.
2. Resource investigator: explores opportunities and contacts.
3. Coordinator: clarifies goals and promotes decision making.
4. Shaper: drives the team forward.
5. Team worker: provides support and encourages cooperation.
6. Monitor evaluator: has discerning judgement.
7. Implementer: turns ideas into action.
8. Completer: has attention to detail.
9. Specialist: has technical knowledge and skills.

Having an awareness of what makes teams successful, the role you play within a team and what might be missing from teams can help you to achieve your goals, especially if your project at work is heavily reliant on the success of the team and therefore the individual successes within. Being able to identify what is missing from a team and developing your skills to fill in the gaps will help you stand apart from the rest and enable group success.

---

3   See https://knowhow.ncvo.org.uk/your-team/people-management-skills/teams/effectiveteam/roles

From the descriptions above, which role do you think you play in a team?

....

Being a good team player means you need a lot of different skills to complement the team you're in and complete the task ahead. You'll need good communication and listening skills, the ability to take responsibility for the parts that you play, and be able to deliver on the tasks that you have agreed to complete within the appropriate timeframes. You'll need the ability to collaborate with others, listen to others' suggestions, to hear and respond appropriately to constructive criticism, and have the drive, motivation and knowledge to complete the tasks.

What skills do you have that make you a good team player?

....

....

....

....

Are there any skills you would like to focus on that will help your development and enhance the teams you're working within?

....

....

....

....

If you're not sure about what further skills you might need, speak to someone you trust, your supervisor or a trusted colleague, and ask for constructive criticism about your skills. Be honest with this person and ask them to tell you the things you might not want to hear. Be open to hearing what you can improve upon. This can be difficult, but without knowing this, you'll struggle to develop and progress. Even if you are certain about the skills you'd like to develop, it is an excellent exercise to ask for constructive feedback from a trusted person within an area of your life that you're wanting to improve on. Write down the feedback you have received here:

....

....

....

....
....
....

Do you agree with the feedback you have been given? If not, why not?

....
....
....
....

What opportunities do you have that will help you to practise and develop your skills?

....
....
....
....

If you haven't got any obvious development opportunities, can you propose an opportunity to your manager/significant person?

....
....

What benefits will this bring to the people/organisation in your life?

....
....
....
....

Is it cost effective?

....

If not, can it be scaled down to a smaller opportunity?

....
....

Who will you speak to and propose/pitch your idea and opportunity?

....

When will you do this by?

....

What was the outcome?

....

....

....

....

If you weren't successful in gaining the opportunity you needed, ask for feedback on why this is not a viable option and write it down here:

....

....

....

....

....

....

With this feedback in mind, what can you change about your idea that will still give you the opportunity to develop but takes your feedback into consideration?

....

....

....

....

Sometimes we don't get the opportunities that we need straight away, but having the ability to receive constructive criticism, and analyse and reflect on it and put a new idea on the table is essential practice for reaching your potential. Not everything is going to go your way all the time, so having the ability to dust yourself off, stand up and try again is crucial to your success.

Initiative

Initiative within the workplace is the ability to analyse, adapt and understand a situation before taking action to resolve a problem or enhance a situation. Using your initiative is not just limited to the workplace but can be used in all areas of your life. It can often save time and resources when executed effectively, for example to prevent a problem from becoming more serious.

Using your own initiative is a key skill to develop; once well practised it becomes a part of you and your life ethos and can help you find solutions to problems, work and develop faster, and help you learn new strategies for success as you try new ways of working and thinking.

To develop your initiative skills requires a lot of practice and an understanding of where the boundaries lie, particularly if you're trying to develop initiative at work. There are some decisions that will have to be made in the workplace by people who are further up the chain than you, so understanding where the boundary of your responsibilities crosses over into others' is essential. To find out where the boundaries lie for you at work, have an open discussion with your line manager. Find out what they want from you in relation to using your initiative. Ask them to give you some examples of when you could have used your initiative. This might be a difficult conversation to spring on someone, so having an initial conversation to prepare your manager might help. This will give them the opportunity to think about your request, gather feedback from others and present their findings back to you.

You can use this as an opportunity to explain that you're looking for this feedback as it is part of your personal development plan, and you'd like to improve your skills. This exercise alone promotes using your initiative and will show your employer that you're serious about developing your skills, enhancing your career and supporting the organisation the best way you can.

If you're not currently in employment, you can do the same activity with anyone else who is reliant on you for your efforts; if you're volunteering, for example, you can speak to your line manager or even your partner or trusted friend.

Write your feedback here:

....

....

....

....

....

....

What opportunities do you have that will enable you to practise using your initiative?

....

....

....

....

When will you do this by?

....

Once you've used your opportunities to use your initiative, don't forget to reflect on your experiences. How did you feel using your own initiative to solve a problem or enhance a situation?

....

....

....

....

....

....

Has this improved your confidence/self-esteem? In what way?

....

....

....

....

Do you feel you can use what you have learnt now to help you in the future? If so, how?

....

....

....

....

How will you make sure that you continue to practise using your initiative?

....

....

....

....

What will this bring to your life that will be positive for you?

....

....

....

....

As you practise using your initiative more and more it will become an integral and natural part of your life. It is a skill that many employers value and will help you in your personal life also.

Solution-focused mindset

Being able to confront an issue that needs resolving – whether in relation to your personal goals, work life or relationships – and find a viable solution is crucial for your success. For example, tackling problems at work with a solution-focused approach is a skill that employers value. The ability to utilise a solution-focused approach as opposed to focusing on a problem helps alleviate and manage stress, and the more practice you have at using a solution-focused approach, the more innovative you will become with your solutions.

Adopting a solution-focused mindset is a strategy you can utilise in every part of your life and is a 'life ethos'. Having the ability to move through your daily life using a solution-focused approach can help you overcome obstacles easier and manage when things become difficult or if you get overwhelmed, and is linked to the small steps approach to life also.

Being solution focused means that you view every obstacle in front of you with a solution-focused mindset. This means that instead of reprimanding people, feeling frustrated or letting other people come up with a solution to the issue, you are actively engaged in overcoming the obstacle yourself or by discussing the solution with others. Having a solution-focused perspective also rubs off on other people. It can help them to promote thinking differently about situations and to alleviate those dark and bogged-down feelings you get when you think there isn't an answer to the problem.

Sometimes there isn't a solution, and that might be the solution. Having the ability to step back from a problem and not let it take up your valuable energy if you cannot change the outcome is a skill that requires practice. It can be incredibly frustrating at times; this affects your mood as well as those around you. Often people around you will pick up your frustrations and negative mindset and this can dig you into a deeper hole, bringing others with you.

Being solution focused isn't necessarily about having a positive mindset; it's about finding practical and appropriate solutions to issues that you may face. It's not about thinking positively; it's about taking action. The actions you take and mindset you have influence others, and if you're working within a team, particularly if you play an essential role within a team such as the team leader, then your mindset and energy will greatly influence the group and the group is likely to match what you bring to the table. So, if you're wanting results and the ability to overcome issues you're facing in any part of your life, then a solution-focused approach is for you.

Let's practise what this would look like for you at work. Think of a problem that you have or have recently experienced and explain it here:

....
....
....
....
....
....

Ask yourself the following questions.

Why has this happened? (Think about this in an operational capacity. This isn't about blaming people; it's about understanding what went wrong and at what point to ensure that you don't make the same mistake twice.)

....
....
....
....
....
....

Have you faced this problem before? Or a problem that was similar? If so, what happened?

....
....
....
....
....
....

How did you solve the problem? What was the solution?

....
....
....
....
....
....

What did you learn about yourself from your previous experience that will help you this time?

....
....
....
....

Will the solution to your previous problem help with this one?

....

If so, explain how:

....
....
....
....
....
....

If not, reflect on the current issue. Identify five things that will help resolve the issue:

1. ....
2. ....
3. ....
4. ....
5. ....

Trying to find five solutions to problems can seem overwhelming and daunting, but once you start to put some time, effort and imagination in, you'll be surprised by what you come up with. When faced with any problem, one of the solutions that might sometimes be most appropriate is to do nothing. If this is the case, make sure you complete the activity to ensure that you're picking the right solution for the issue you're facing – informed decisions are the best decisions!

For one of the above solutions you have thought of, identify the consequences of your solution. Think about what the benefits will be, how this will affect you, the organisation or the people around you and whether there will be any negative consequences as well as positive consequences:

....
....
....
....
....
....
....
....
....
....
....
....

Take each of your possible solutions one by one and repeat the exercise.

Sometimes there is no such thing as a perfect solution to issues; other times it's straightforward, and the answer might be staring you in the face. However, practising going through this process for even the simplest of issues you're facing will encourage you to be able to remember its steps so you can repeat them quickly in your day-to-day life, enabling you to make faster decisions and find solutions much more easily.

What is the solution that you have decided to take for the issue you are facing?

....

....

....

....

And finally, does this decision align itself with your personal values?

....

Think back to the start of the book where you identified what was most important to you in respect of your values. Ensuring your decisions and solutions align with your values will give you confidence in the decision-making process and ensure that you're living your life being true to yourself.

Sometimes you'll come across someone – and everyone will have this experience at some time – who points out the problem and then all the potential barriers linked to the problem that you'll face; but they won't attempt to bring a solution. You can find yourself in meetings that last for hours where someone complains about what's happened and the impact on the business and themselves. However, when anyone else brings up a possible solution, they dismiss it and point out all the problems with that solution. When you're on the receiving end of people like that, how does it make you feel?

....

....

....

....

Energy from others, particularly negative energy, can have a big impact on others; positive people who express positive energy and have solution-focused lifestyles are easy to be around. Think about a person who responds to life with a solution-focused and positive mindset. When you're around them, how does this impact you? How do you feel when you're with them and hear them speak?

....
....
....
....

Which of the two do you prefer – those who express negative energy or those who give out positive energy?

....

Why?

....
....
....
....

Who would you rather emulate?

....

Why?

....
....
....
....

You can see there are very clear differences between the two approaches to problems, and the impact that those two examples have on you and others can be the difference between thriving at work and life or just complaining about work and life, feeling helpless to change things for the better.

SNAPSHOT

📷 Understanding where you are now in your career, having an ambitious plan and working backwards to develop smaller step-by-step goals will help you achieve your dreams!

- Developing your individual skills will enhance your performance as an individual but will also have a knock-on effect on your wider team.
- Teamwork is the essence of all we do in life. Understanding your contributions to a team and how you can build on your teamwork skills will lead to more successes and collective achievements within team environments.
- Having a solution-focused mindset isn't about 'thinking positively'; it's about choosing to focus on the end goal by implementing solutions to overcome barriers, leading to your successes!
- Being solution focused can help to reduce stress and worry by focusing on what the next step is going to be rather than dwelling on the situation.

• Chapter 9 •

Performance

Humans are incredibly powerful as a species but it's important to understand that the species is made up of individual and incredible people at its heart. You have the power and potential to achieve whatever you set your mind to. You can enhance your life and progress towards your personal goals – leading to significant personal achievements in every area of your life. Having the ability to understand how powerful you are as an individual can influence others towards collective and societal change, can bring fulfilment and happiness to your life and can change the world – it's all in the actions you take and the responses you have to your life events and trajectory.

There are many different strategies you can use to your advantage to enhance your daily performance. They can be used alongside the strategies that you have learnt in the other chapters or to develop self-management skills and achieve your goals! Having the ability to understand your own personal power and using that to influence your day-to-day performance will uncover a world of opportunities and lifetime achievements that you might never have thought possible.

If we take a tiny step towards change or improvement in any area of our life every single day, the cumulative result over a year is significant – every tiny step is one step towards your goals, and once you've achieved what you set out to initially, you'll see that these tiny steps add up to huge leaps towards your preferred future.

Imposter syndrome

One of the biggest issues that holds people back from achieving their goals is imposter syndrome. The Oxford English Dictionary defines it as follows: 'The persistent inability to believe that one's success is deserved or has been legitimately achieved as a result of one's own efforts or skills.'

Imposter syndrome is the belief that all your hard work on your personal development, career goals or in any other area of your life isn't yours to own: that you 'cheated' somehow, or it was 'too easy', therefore anyone could have done what you did. This is something that you should be aware of especially as you move through your small steps and reach your ultimate goals. Owning your achievements and taking credit for the effort that you put in to obtaining them is essential to your continued success. If you're not aware of the dangers of imposter syndrome, it can catch you out and affect your self-esteem and confidence, and can sometimes lead you to give up on progressing towards your goals.

Imposter syndrome can sneak up on people because it can bubble under the surface of your consciousness: that tiny voice that tells you, despite all your hard work, 'Anyone could have done that', or that reminds you that the skills you have are not exclusive to you and you're not that special. Having an awareness of imposter syndrome and how it manifests itself is crucial to your future successes; understanding how to manage imposter syndrome (just as you've learnt to manage and overcome other obstacles) is essential to ensuring that you don't trivialise your achievements and that you celebrate your hard work and dedication to your personal goals.

Throughout this book we've seen the importance of reviewing your progress to help you learn from your experiences and celebrate your achievements. Reviewing your progress can help you manage imposter syndrome as it enables you to focus on what went well and areas for improvement.

Many people who embark upon journeys to self-improvement and better futures often stumble into imposter syndrome, but if you're not aware of it, that's when it can hit you the hardest! Knowing about potential stumbling blocks can help you to identify what's happening to you and to put some strategies in place to manage it.

Reflecting on previous experiences, has there ever been a time when you've felt the sting of imposter syndrome? Explain what happened:

....

....

....

....

....

....

How did it make you feel?

....

....

....

....

How did this experience impact your life?

....

....

....

....

Did you recognise it as imposter syndrome at the time? If not, can you explain why not?

....

....

....

....

Looking back on this experience now, knowing about imposter syndrome, is there anything you could have put in place or done differently to mitigate the impact?

....

....

....

....

....

....

Many of the strategies in the self-esteem and confidence chapter can be used to mitigate the impact of imposter syndrome. Imposter syndrome can regularly occur when you've been working hard for something over a long period of time that can be considered one of your biggest achievements. That's when it's crucial to reflect on your hard work and accomplishments and take credit for what you did.

Reflect on an achievement you accomplished where you didn't necessarily give yourself the credit you deserved. What happened? What did you achieve?

....

....

....
....
....
....

How did you achieve this? (Think about your personal contribution and efforts.)

....
....
....
....
....
....

Was this something you found easy?

....

What were you most proud of in this situation?

....
....
....
....

Was there a time you wanted to give up? Describe the situation here:

....
....
....
....
....
....

What would have happened if you had given up?

....
....

....

....

Having reflected on this experience, what do you want to say to yourself now that you didn't at the time?

....

....

....

....

Use this exercise to reflect after any achievement you feel is significant to your progress (either big or small!) and make sure you positively reflect on the effort that you put in to achieve that goal, instead of waiting a few months or years to take pride in your achievement.

Commemorating your achievements can also help; for instance, taking and presenting photos in your home of key events in your life will help you to remember the hard work you've put in, especially when you go on to achieve more in your life. You'll be able to look back on these memories and draw on what you learnt to enable you to reach your next achievement.

Prioritisation

Effectively being able to prioritise your life is what will separate you from those who achieve what they set out to and those that continue their status quo. If partying with your friends is top of the agenda and you don't put aside some time for your development, then you'll maintain your status quo. If you set aside some time to work on your goals or projects and take small steps towards your preferred future, you'll eventually get where you want to be. Being able to take yourself and your development seriously is what will set you aside from the rest and will encourage you to reach your full potential. In Chapter 8 we discussed how Eisenhower's matrix can be used to prioritise your workload, but it can also be applied to other areas of your life such as:

Health	Relationships	Spiritual	Intellectual
Career	Self-esteem	Financial	Friendship
Business	Confidence	Community	Romance

Using the matrix to understand what is urgent and most important for you and not urgent and not important right now, identify the top three areas of your life to start working on now:

1. ....

2. ....

3. ....

Use the strategies you've learnt throughout this book to start setting yourself some goals, working backwards to identify small steps, and set aside some time to put some effort and work into achieving them.

Other ways to support you to prioritise your life are to use 'to do lists'. These can be used in many forms, daily, weekly or even monthly, but the principle is the same. Write down your priorities for the day/week/month and work through your list – doing the most important tasks first. Crossing items off can be incredibly satisfying and helps to show you that you are making progress. To do lists can be used in all areas of your life, from work life to home life and everything in between, and are an effective way to ensure that you don't forget any tasks you need to do, helping to manage your time more effectively.

Procrastination

This is one of the biggest barriers to achieving your goals. You can end up procrastinating because you can't quite face what's ahead of you or there's too much for you to do, so you become overwhelmed and don't even start your list of tasks. This ends in a vicious cycle of never starting the list and it continuing to get longer. Similar principles to the other areas we've discussed apply here: small steps approaches and breaking everything down into smaller, more manageable chunks.

For example, perhaps you were planning on going for a run but you're tired and it's raining. You know you should go, and you know you'll feel better afterwards, but you're still procrastinating even though it's been playing on your mind for hours on end. If you'd have bitten the bullet and gone out there and then, your mind would be freed up to think about other things and you'd be able to invest your time in other tasks/activities. Thinking about the whole run, how far it is, how the weather is and so on has made you feel more and more overwhelmed, so it takes you hours to get out there.

Breaking this down into smaller steps can help. By only focusing on the next smallest step – for example, nothing more than getting changed into your running clothes – then once you've completed that focusing on the next smallest step – getting your running shoes on and gathering what you need to take with you – you're much more likely to reach the final step of getting your feet out of the front door. Usually, the first step with anything is the hardest, so focusing on taking the first step and thinking less on the bigger picture can help you achieve more, free up your mind and in situations like this example, once you've got your feet out of the door the rest will follow, and you'll be off on your run and back home for a shower before you know it! Take the first smallest step towards anything you're facing to prevent wandering around thinking about doing things, feeling guilty for not doing them and wasting the day by thinking about all the things you should do but then don't.

Becoming aware that you're procrastinating and drawing attention to that in your mind can also help to reduce the amount of procrastinating you're doing. If you know you need to do something and you become aware that you're procrastinating, take the first smallest step and then stop what you are doing. Take the next smallest step, which is to review your tasks for the day and start one of them. Break down the task that you have chosen to do into even smaller steps and complete each step methodically. You'll soon gain momentum with your daily tasks and before you know it, will have completed what you set out to achieve for the day. Once you start to become productive in the day, you'll start to become motivated to achieve a little bit more than you had originally planned in the first instance. Practising living in the moment and only focusing on what you're doing in any given moment will support you on your path to being more productive by drawing awareness to your procrastinating habits.

Setting aside some time every morning to write a list of what you want to achieve each day – a list that is SMART – will help prevent procrastination. Motivate yourself by having something to look forward to each day if you complete your tasks. This might be to spend some time doing something you love or just hanging out with friends, family or loved ones. Having a reward for yourself after completing mundane tasks can help to motivate you to complete them so you can get on with the things you enjoy.

Reframing your tasks is also a good strategy to use to help prevent procrastination. Understanding the benefits of why you're completing certain tasks and seeing the wider benefits of doing them can help give purpose to what you're doing. For example, take an everyday task such as washing the dishes. It's not the most exciting job in the world, but it's something that needs to be done. Reframing this as a task done to serve others or a task completed so that you can cook something lovely later (if you like cooking!) can help put a different perspective on the task and help you feel more motivated to complete it. If you're supporting a family, washing the dishes has a positive impact on everyone in the home including yourself. You can reframe the running example by thinking about the benefits this brings to your life and how it's an act of self-care to help you be the best version of yourself every day – rather than focusing on how cold and wet it is outside.

Try to understand the reasons why you are procrastinating. If it's because you don't want to do the task ahead of you but it must be done, completing it faster will mean it's out of your mind and away from your focus much quicker than it would be if you procrastinate and therefore dwell on the fact that you've still got to do it, even though hours have passed. Use your time better by finishing the task first so it's out of the way and you can enjoy spending time doing the things you want to do rather than the things you have to do.

Think about a task that's been on your to do list for a long time. Why haven't you completed it yet?

....

....

....

....

What impact is not doing the task having on your life?

....

....

....

....

How is this making you feel?

....

....

If you completed this task tomorrow, what benefits would this bring to your life? How would you feel?

....

....

....

....

Is there anything you need to prepare first to complete the task?

....

....

By completing the task, would this benefit anyone else in your life?

....

If so, how?

....

....

What is the first smallest step that you need to complete to start the task?

....

....

When could you do this first step by?

....

Having completed the first smallest step, how do you feel now?

....

....

Approximately how much time did you spend thinking about completing the task but not acting on it?

....

Approximately how long did it take you to complete the first smallest step?

....

Approximately how long did it take you to complete the task?

....

Think about the time that you have spent thinking about completing the task vs the time you've spent completing the task. Was there a significant difference between the two?

....

What else could you have done with the time you spent thinking about the task, if you had completed it and not procrastinated?

....

....

Would this have brought more benefits to your life?

....

....

You can use this reflections exercise to help you become motivated to complete a task. It takes minutes to complete and will help you to complete the task at hand, which is more beneficial than spending hours thinking about doing the task but not doing it. Finding ways like this to help you logically motivate yourself into action can save you time in the long run – so you can spend time doing things you like!

> **TOP TIP**
> Switch off or put away anything that is distracting you from what you need to complete for the day. If it's there and in your face, you're more likely to engage with it.

Productivity

Increasing your productivity with the time that you do have is another approach to helping you to achieve your personal and life goals faster. The more productive you are with your time, the faster you will make progress towards your preferred future. Many people lead busy lives and it's easy to feel that there isn't time to do anything other than what you're already doing. Having a good daily routine, being prepared, getting enough sleep, eating well and exercising will all help you feel like you have more energy to take on a few additional tasks a day to help you strive towards your preferred future.

Having more energy and sleeping well will give you the strength to get up a little bit earlier every day. By getting up even ten minutes earlier in the morning, you will have ten extra minutes every day to do something you either need or want to do. You could spend these ten minutes meditating, writing your lists, prioritising your tasks or to give yourself enough time to make breakfast instead of skipping it. You can get up as early as you want to give yourself those additional minutes of the day to complete what you want to. You could get up half an hour earlier every day and use this time as your personal development time, to write that job application, read that book, prepare yourself for the day or go for a run! The world is a quieter place in the morning, before everyone else gets up and the chaos of rush hour traffic and working lives ensues.

Having some extra time in the morning to centre yourself, prepare for the day ahead and complete some tasks will not only ensure you become more productive, but it will also give you a sense of achievement before you've even got out of the door. Starting the day with purpose also sets you up with the right attitude for the day, helps you become more productive throughout the day, which can keep stress at bay and, again, gives you that little bit of additional time to propel yourself towards your preferred future.

Getting up a little bit earlier each day and training yourself to do so takes some time, but by starting small with just 10 minutes and building this up to 30 minutes or even an hour, you'll slowly build up to a routine that works for you, and this is one of the easiest ways to maximise your productivity with very little effort on your part – other than actually getting out of bed a little earlier! As we've discussed in the procrastination section, once you've taken that first step, you're more likely to complete the tasks you set out to; make getting out of bed 10 minutes earlier your first smallest step.

TOP TIP

Write down what you want to achieve with your extra morning time the night before, so you're focused and make the most of the additional time you've given yourself.

Setting yourself some personal boundaries will also help you to become more productive. You can use this technique in any area of your life where you need to be a little stricter with the time that you have. A good example of setting yourself boundaries would be to limit the time you spend on your work emails throughout the day. The constant ping of the email notifications distracts you from any project or task you have to do and cuts down the time that you are actually productive if you're constantly answering emails throughout the day; this is especially true if you're answering emails that seem like 'quick wins' and make you feel productive. When you're answering the quick-win emails that could have waited for another time, you're taking time away from the project that you need to complete and have a strict deadline for.

If you're worried about missing emails that might be urgent, set your out of office to reply with your phone number in case of an emergency. The recipient can then call you if their email is truly urgent and requires your attention immediately. Limiting yourself to checking your emails twice a day – in the morning and in the afternoon – can help you become more productive. You can answer those quick wins first thing in the morning, which will make you feel you've achieved something very early on in the day, and that in itself is a great strategy for motivation. You can then check your emails again later in the afternoon before you finish work; this can help you prioritise your emails and work for the following day. As we've discussed in other sections, prioritising and organising tasks or work you must do leads to higher levels of productivity and higher levels of personal satisfaction at having achieved some of the tasks on your to do list.

Setting personal boundaries can be done in any area of your life. For example, perhaps you spend too much time on your phone scrolling through social media or you spend too much time gaming. Set yourself weekly or daily limits that will help you make the most of your time. There's nothing wrong with switching off by playing video games or connecting with others and seeing content on social media, but when this bleeds into spending most of your time outside of work on social media or games consoles, that's when you'll struggle to achieve your personal goals. Limiting the time spent on activities like this will give you more time for personal development or to complete that task you've been putting off for weeks!

Think about some of the habits in your life that, if you limited your time on them, could give you more time to do other tasks or work on your personal development. What are these?

....
....
....
....
....
....

Choose one habit and work out how much time you spend doing it every day/week/month:

....
....

How does spending this much time affect your day-to-day life?

....

....

....

....

How does that make you feel?

....

....

....

....

If you weren't doing this activity, what could you spend your time on instead that would help you progress towards meeting your personal and life goals?

....

....

What benefit would this bring to your life?

....

....

Thinking back to how you're spending your time, what would be a reasonable amount of time to spend on the activity you've chosen?

....

Can this be easily implemented?

....

How can you ensure you put these boundaries in place for yourself?

....

....

....

....

What personal rules are you going to commit to that will help you limit your time on the activity?

....

....

....

....

Can anyone support you with this?

....

....

....

....

Many apps and games now have timer devices whereby you can set personal limits on them and after you've exceeded your time for the day the app will lock you out of it. This can help support you on your journey to being more productive. It is also a good reminder to complete any tasks you've not yet done for the day as the app will kick you out and that will leave you with some time on your hands to complete your to do list.

Chunking is an excellent strategy to implement the small steps approach on a micro level. Chunking is splitting up your day into half-hour chunks and working within those timeframes to achieve more with your time. Split up your day into half-hour chunks and schedule your tasks into those chunks. By seeing your time in chunks, you can see what time you do have and become more efficient. This is also beneficial throughout the working day if you have multiple tasks to complete but are feeling overwhelmed. When you are starting a task in the half an hour you have, you should focus solely on that task, ignoring distractions, not doing any side tasks and being in the moment. Remember to schedule breaks in too – rest and recuperation are just as important as being productive and, as discussed in previous sections, can help you become more productive. Try this template to get you started:

06:30		15:00	
07:00		15:30	
07:30		16:00	
08:00		16:30	

08:30		17:00	
09:00		17:30	
09:30		18:00	
10:00		18:30	
10:30		19:00	
11:00		19:30	
11:30		20:00	
12:00		20:30	
12:30		21:00	
13:00		21:30	
13:30		22:00	
14:00		22:30	
14:30		23:00	

This strategy can also be used to help you get up half an hour earlier and use that half an hour productively – you can even split it up further into 15-minute chunks if that works better for you.

TOP TIP

Try different strategies to see what makes you most productive.

Overall wellbeing

Your overall wellbeing will determine how quickly you reach and exceed your goals. As discussed in the chapter on health, having a healthy lifestyle can accelerate your progress as you'll have more energy and you'll be eating and sleeping better, which helps brain function and keeps you performing at your best. Other activities you can incorporate into your life that have proven benefits for your overall wellbeing are yoga, meditation, journaling and learning.

There are many resources online to help you get started with yoga and meditation from free courses on YouTube to downloadable PDFs – all it takes is a little bit of research to find some resources that you can incorporate into your daily routine. Learning about activities such as a yoga, meditation and journaling can also help you on your journey and means you've spent some time learning too – learning should form part of any personal development journey. Now it's time to put it into practice.

These activities are not for everyone, but it's important to try new things to determine whether they will bring benefits to your life and if you will enjoy spending time participating in them – people who do yoga, meditation, journaling or any other wellbeing activity all started somewhere and were all new to it at one point, so don't be put off joining a class or reaching out to experts in your community for advice and support in starting. If joining a class works better for you then research your local offers for beginners.

Best of all yoga and meditation can be free, they don't need any equipment (apart from initial resources to learn how to practise) and can be done at home or anywhere else in the world! There are many apps you can download to support you with guided meditation and many courses that you can do either online or in person; it's just a case of finding out what is available to you with the resources you have.

Yoga has many benefits including stress relief, reducing inflammation, improving flexibility and reducing anxiety – these are all things that will benefit your life and bring a sense of positive wellbeing and enrichment. Meditation can support you with being in the moment, which we have discussed throughout this book – this will help you enjoy your personal development journey and focus on the steps rather than the overall goal. Happiness isn't reserved for when you reach your final goal; personal development journeys should be enjoyed every step of the way, and if you're not enjoying it, something needs to change. Maybe you need to re-evaluate your goals.

Meditation can also help to reduce stress and negative emotions, increase your patience and tolerance and increase your self-awareness.[1] The more self-aware you are on your personal development journey, the better skilled you will be at understanding your potential and identifying what you need to help you reach your goals and when you need to change or adjust your goals to reach your preferred future. As you can see, meditation and yoga can have life-changing positive effects, but don't just take my word for it – do your own research and make that a part of your learning journey.

Reading and journaling also have health benefits.[2] Spending time reading to learn new things or even for pleasure can decrease depression, lower your blood pressure and heart rate, aid sleep readiness (we've all heard the tip to read before we go to bed!), improve brain connectivity, and increase your vocabulary and comprehension. Reading to learn will help give you the knowledge and understanding of your chosen subjects, and if you're trying to take those next steps with any of your goals, will enhance that process for you. So, it's good for your health and for

---

1   www.mayoclinic.org/tests-procedures/meditation/in-depth/meditation/art-20045858
2   www.healthline.com/health/benefits-of-reading-books

reaching your goals. If reading isn't your thing, try listening to audio books; whilst it has different benefits to reading, you'll still have a whole host of entertaining stories and knowledge at your fingertips!

Journaling and reflecting on your days will help you to learn new things about yourself and to reflect on your achievements, which in turn will help you see the progress you are making towards your goals. You will have also documented your life and its achievements, and when you look back on this it can be incredibly rewarding and motivating.

Build your own personal wellbeing routine by incorporating the strategies discussed in this book – don't overcommit; try one new thing a month or commit to one thing for three months instead, and that will give you enough data to reflect on whether you think it will work for you long term. Enjoy the journey. You'll learn a lot about yourself from participating in activities such as yoga, meditation, journaling and reading.

SNAPSHOT

- Increase your productivity and reduce your procrastination to enable progress towards your personal goals.
- The performance tools are just that – tools to help you on your journey towards a preferred future. Pick the ones that work best for you – everyone is different.
- Accelerate your motivation by incorporating healthy wellbeing habits such as yoga, meditation, journaling and learning.
- Learning will help you progress towards your goals faster; having a willingness to increase your knowledge, particularly if that knowledge is associated with your personal goals, will help you on your journey.
- Self-management skills will enable you to manage your life, manage stress, anxiety and depression, and keep you performing at your best.
- Try something new!

Conclusion

In the second chapter of this book, you completed an exercise that was designed to understand where you were at with each of the areas covered in this book to gain an understanding of what you wanted to focus on. Using the same model, identify where you are now on each of the sections below by marking yourself on a scale of 1 to 6, where 1 means you are not happy in this area at all and 6 means you're completely fulfilled in this area of your life.

Where are you now?

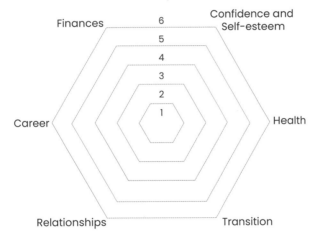

Mark where you are on each section with a cross. Connect the crosses with a single line. Is there a difference in progress from when you first did this exercise?

....

....

How do you feel about what you have achieved?

....

....

....

....

On reflection, what has this process taught you?

....

....

....

....

....

....

....

....

....

....

....

....

Congratulate yourself on your progress – reward yourself too! Don't underestimate the effort that you have made towards reaching your personal goals and how much time and commitment it takes, as well as bravery, to look within yourself and challenge yourself to reach your preferred future.

The strategies you have learnt throughout this book will give you different ways in which to achieve your goals based on what will work best for you. They will help you on your journey to your preferred future and make up the way in which you manage yourself and your time. Effective self-management is the key to your future successes, because without having self-management tools you'll start projects or journeys but struggle to reach your goals. You must have a set of self-management skills to enable the strategies to be useful for you. These include effective time management, motivation to get up and do what you said you were going to do, the ability to achieve your daily tasks on the days when you don't want to, and not overstretching yourself to a point where your goals and tasks become unmanageable – you cannot be all things to all people all the time.

Streamlining your life with the techniques as discussed in the chapter on performance and becoming organised and motivated will help you achieve your goals. Ultimately, you could try every strategy in this book, but without consistency and commitment you won't achieve your goals. Small steps continuously and consistently are what will help you reach your full potential. It doesn't matter how long it takes you to get to where you want to go; all that matters is that you progress a tiny bit every single day.

Some days will be better than others; some days will be easier than others. But it's the days that you don't want to complete your personal development tasks that will matter the most. Those are the days that will help you build resilience and awareness of the strength you have and will propel you forward to reach your goals. The challenges you face and how you manage them, working round the obstacles step by step, will shape your future.

Ultimately, the only person that will ensure you reach your goals is you. There are no quick fixes; there are no one-week programmes that will help you achieve your long-term goals. These programmes are good for kick-starting new beginnings or to help you in the short term but are sometimes not sustainable. Hard work, determination, motivation to succeed and a long-term commitment to making tiny steps of progress every single day are what will give you your preferred future.

Yearly reviews can help support your progress by getting you to reflect on your achievements. You'll be able to see how far you've come in a relatively short space of time (in the context of the average life span). Seeing what you have achieved over a year can help you identify any future goals you want to achieve as well as celebrating what you have done already. We can often forget what we have achieved over time, so having a journal identifying your achievements is a great way to look back on what you've done over the years and can help you gain strength on those demotivated days or when you want to throw in the towel and go back to old habits!

The most important thing to remember is that it doesn't matter whether you're trying to slightly improve your lifestyle by getting more sleep or eating better, or if you're going for a big promotion or business launch. What matters is that your goals are personal to you and reflect where you want to be, and that you ensure you commit to getting there. Anything is possible with the right tools, support and attitude to change. So – plan, try out different strategies and find what works for you, be organised with your time, make SMART goals, don't overcommit and start working on your personal development now. There's no time like the present and your future self will thank you.

Acknowledgements

There are far too many people that have helped me achieve my preferred future to mention by name, but they know who they are. I am incredibly grateful to, first and foremost, my family who have always encouraged me to do my best and pushed me to take opportunities that have been afforded to me.

I'd like to thank my friends, who have supported me through challenging times, and continued to cheer me on when I've shared my goals with them, who've been there through the good, the bad and the ugly. It's been a wild ride already, and I'm looking forward to where the years take us next. Their friendship and kindness are incredibly valuable to me, and I wouldn't have achieved half the things I have done without them.

I have been blessed to have met some incredible people in my life already. Thank you to the many teachers, youth workers, mentors, coaches, supervisors, managers, employers, colleagues and peers who have been extremely generous with their time and have shared their experiences and expertise with me over the years. Their support has helped me to learn and develop and has pushed me to achieve things I never thought possible. Their seemingly endless reserves of patience, kindness and generosity have enabled me to have rich and diverse learning experiences that have had a profound impact on my life.

To the team at Jessica Kingsley Publishers who have supported me to write this book and my previous publication: thank you for giving me the opportunity to share my knowledge with the world. You've helped me to achieve a lifelong dream.

And most importantly, thank you to my partner Kathy, who no matter what strange and bizarre idea I come up with for my next challenge or adventure, always supports me, encourages me and is there for me. Her companionship and love are a gift beyond measure.